Called to Prayer

CALLED TO PRAYER

LITURGICAL SPIRITUALITY TODAY

Gerard Austin, O.P.
Theresa F. Koernke, I.H.M.
Mary Collins, O.S.B.
Louis Weil

THE LITURGICAL PRESS
St. John's Abbey • Collegeville, MN 56321

Cover design by Mary Jo Pauly

Grateful acknowledgement is made to the Macmillan Publishing Company, London and Basingstoke, England, for permission to reprint "The Bright Field" from *Later Poems 1972–1982* by R. S. Thomas.

THE LITURGICAL PRESS
Collegeville, Minnesota 56321

1	2	3	4	5	6	7	8	9

Library of Congress Cataloging-in-Publication Data

Federation of Diocesan Liturgical Commissions.
   National Meeting (1985 : Grand Rapids, Mich.)
   Called to prayer.
   Sponsored by the Federation of Diocesan Liturgical Commissions and the Bishops' Committee on the Liturgy.
   1. Catholic Church—Liturgy—Congresses.
2. Spirituality—Catholic Church—Congresses.
3. Catholic Church—Doctrines—Congresses.
I. Austin, Gerard. II. Johnson, Lawrence J., 1933-
III. Federation of Diocesan Liturgical Commissions.
IV. Catholic Church. National Conference of Catholic Bishops. Bishops' Committee on the Liturgy.
BX1970.A1F43 1985   264'.02   86-15365
ISBN 0-8146-1488-4

Contents

Foreword

Throughout the past two decades significant modifications have characterized the life and worship of the Christian community. These touch upon the manner in which we view our relationships with God, with others, and with all of creation. They affect the way we mold our religious attitudes and express our piety. They relate to our understanding of what it means to live as Christians. They extend to our forms and methods of prayer. Our response to God's saving Word has been reshaped, often dramatically, by the renewal efforts within the Christian community at large and within the Roman Catholic community in particular.

Although liturgical practice does not exhaust the meaning of the gospel message, the way a Church prays together mirrors and uniquely expresses the totality of its life and faith. To explore some of the spiritual implications of recent liturgical renewal within the Roman Church was the purpose of the October 1985 National Meeting of Diocesan Liturgical Commissions, sponsored by the Federation of Diocesan Liturgical Commissions and the Bishops' Committee on the Liturgy. The theme of the gathering, held in Grand Rapids, Michigan, was "Liturgical Spirituality: Faith Shaping Prayer Shaping Faith." This volume contains the four major addresses given on that occasion.

In the opening address, "Spirit Through Word," Fr. Gerard Austin, O.P., explores how the relationship between Word and sacrament can best be understood within the context of the role of the Spirit. It is through the Word that the community gathers in the Spirit who brings about the Eucharistic mystery. God's spoken Word is completely embodied in the Eucharist. Thus, says Father Austin, there is a great danger in casually accepting Sunday celebrations which lack the totality of the Eucharistic action. Father Austin then presents several challenging insights into the present lectionary reform, the role of the homilist, and the ecumenical advantages of the Common Lectionary.

Sr. Theresa Koernke, I.H.M., addresses the societal implications of worship in "Sacraments: For the Peace and Salvation of All the World." Cautioning against viewing liturgical renewal and social action as entities running on two separate although parallel tracks, she shows that the Church's public worship is the source of Christian behavior. It is through baptism that we have been joined to the Lord Jesus who "is the Justice of God, and we live in that Justice, in that One Liturgy." This, Sister Theresa recalls, is not a "feeling"; rather, it is a given, "not something to be worked for, but recognized even when we do not feel it," a truth having profound implications for liturgical celebration.

Recent years have witnessed the growth of various devotional practices and renewal movements within Christianity. Sr. Mary Collins, O.S.B., addresses this phenomenon in "Devotions and Renewal Movements: Spiritual Cousins of the Liturgy." Using devotion to the Sacred Heart as an illustrative example of the interaction between liturgy, devotions, and renewal movements, she shows that these are currents of the one faith. Human concerns, differing according to times and places, give rise to various devotional expressions and are in turn tested by the traditional living faith. Sister urges liturgical leaders to be alert to such concerns and their popular religious manifestations, to commit themselves "to the affirmation of beauty and the reverence for reality, animate and inanimate," and to "look again at the structure of our lectionary and the support it does or does not provide for new religious sensibility and growing piety."

The role of the arts as essential to the corporate worship experience has been increasingly highlighted within recent years. Nevertheless, artistic creativity remains a problematic dimension for many communities. In "The Arts: Language of the Spirit," Fr. Louis Weil recalls that creative beauty is generated by the work of the Spirit, and yet our inherited models of worship in the West have so tamed the arts that "the fresh springs of creativity are effectively excluded from the liturgical act." He reminds us that pre-packaged models are inimical to the liberating work of the Spirit operative among the members of the local Church. We must be open to the artistic act and the nature of the experience it engenders. We must, he says, be "stewards" of the liturgy. We are called to promote growth. We are to see the "whole created, physical world (as) the resource for the Church's liturgical experience."

The Federation of Diocesan Liturgical Commissions expresses its appreciation to The Liturgical Press for publishing these addresses.

Lawrence J. Johnson
Executive Secretary
Federation of Diocesan Liturgical Commissions

1

Spirit Through Word

GERARD AUSTIN, O.P.

My topic, "Spirit Through Word," is the first presentation of the overall theme "Liturgical Spirituality: Faith Shaping Prayer Shaping Faith." It is very fitting in such a context that we begin with the Word of God and the role that that Word plays in shaping liturgical spirituality.

Granted a certain case can be made for the independent developments in their origins of the liturgy of the Word (the *synaxsis* or "meeting") and the liturgy of the Eucharist (the *eucharistia* or "thanksgiving")[1]; nevertheless, the two have been together for centuries. They are inseparable and form but one reality. The Constitution on the Sacred Liturgy sets this out quite clearly in paragraph 56:

> The two parts that, in a certain sense, go to make up the Mass, namely the liturgy of the word and the liturgy of the eucharist, are so closely connected with each other that they form but one single act of worship.

Thus, gone are the days when we taught people, as I was taught in my youth, that the three essential parts of the

11

Mass are the offertory, consecration, and Communion and that you did not miss Mass as long as you arrived by the offertory. Gone, too, is the use of that curious term, the "fore-Mass," to refer to the Liturgy of the Word. We have humbly come to see that some of the objections of the Protestant reformers were quite valid, and that the Liturgy of the Word has an integrity of its own; but an integrity that is in itself ordered to the Eucharist.

Relationship Between Word and Eucharist

The Constitution on the Sacred Liturgy of Vatican II was prepared for in various ways. One way was the role of international liturgical meetings and congresses like this one taking place in Grand Rapids this week. In 1958 there took place in France the Strasbourg Congress on the theme "The Liturgy and the Word of God." In one of the addresses the Dominican Fr. A. M. Roguet stated:

> Far from being removed from words, the Eucharist requires the Word, the proclamation of the wonderful works of God, the preaching of Christ, the announcement of his passion and resurrection, the promulgation of the Covenant. The Liturgy of the Word is required of the Eucharistic celebration; without the Liturgy of the Word, the Eucharistic celebration is incomplete, it runs the risk of turning into a kind of magic. [2]

This is particularly the case if one over emphasizes the moment of consecration. But this has even broader application as we did that pinpointing of sacramental moments with sacraments other than just the Eucharist. Take baptism, for example. Aidan Kavanagh writes:

> It must be remembered that the baptism of Christians was not Johannine, but Christic: it was a baptism not of water but of Holy Spirit. The water bath is a function of the Spirit. This means that pneumatic data concerning Christian bap-

tism subordinate water data: the latter are to be understood in terms of the former.[3]

Haven't we really forgotten that in the Western Church we actually turned it all around and subordinated Spirit to water? Our attention has been more riveted on the pouring of the water than on giving attention to the gifts of the Spirit. Our tendency to baptize infants of even uncommitted Christian parents said a good deal in this regard. This unfortunate subordination of Spirit to water had a key role in eventually causing the disintegration of our once unified rite of initiation. It also played a key role in our theologizing about baptism more from the point of view of infant baptism than from the point of view of adult baptism.

But to go back to the Eucharist and Father Roguet at the Strasbourg Congress, he said: "The liturgy of the Word is Eucharistic in the proper sense of the word. That is to say, it is not only an instruction meant for the faithful, but also a thanksgiving addressed to God."[4]

The Liturgy of the Word does have a didactic function, but it must not be seen as primarily so. This is an important point because when we view the Mass (especially the readings and the homily) as *chiefly* a time for instruction of our people, we are selling short the Liturgy of the Word. Just as the Eucharist presupposes a *reconciled* community, so the Eucharist presupposes a *catechetized* community. We mustn't make the Mass bear the burden of other things that should be going on in our parish communities: prayer groups, Bible studies, Scripture sharings, adult education groups, etc. The Mass is a time for already instructed people to gather together to praise and thank their God.

The Liturgy of the Word is Eucharistic; it is itself a thanksgiving addressed to God. We recount the wonderful works of God, and in proclaiming them we praise and thank the God who wrought them and who continues to bring them about now, here in our midst.

The Liturgy of the Word itself is an *anamnesis*, a memorial. By the cycle of readings we view not only particular *mirabilia Dei*, but the permanent and universal wonders perceived and remembered above all by the consciousness of the community itself. In this context the community does more than hear the Word of God; it is penetrated by it, transformed by it, because the same God of wonders continues to work in this particular gathered community. The Liturgy of the Word is in that sense an *epiclesis*, an invocation of the Spirit upon the community: that it might continue in time and space the wonderful works of God.

We can well profit from Jewish piety in this regard. For Israel, the Word of God is the Word of the Almighty, it produces what it proclaims by its own power.[5] Isaiah bears witness to this:

> For as the rain and the snow come down from heaven,
>   and return not thither but water the earth,
> making it bring forth and sprout,
>   giving seed to the sower and bread to the eater,
> so shall my word be that goes forth from my mouth;
>   it shall not return to me empty,
> but it shall accomplish that which I purpose,
>   and prosper in the thing for which I sent it (55:10-11).

The Word of God is a fruitful Word. The Breath, the Spirit of God *is* the Action of God.[6] God's Word is a Spirit-filled Word, and in the context of the Mass, this means that the Word, by its very nature, leads us to the Eucharist.

In paragraph 10 of the *Praenotanda*, the Introduction of the 1981 *Ordo Lectionum Missae*, we read:

> The Church is nourished spiritually at the table of God's word and at the table of the eucharist: from the one it grows in wis-

dom and from the other in holiness. In the word of God the divine covenant is announced; in the eucharist the new and everlasting covenant is renewed. The spoken word of God brings to mind the history of salvation; the eucharist embodies it in the sacramental signs of the liturgy. It can never be forgotten, therefore, that the divine word read and proclaimed by the Church in the liturgy has as its one goal the sacrifice of the new Covenant and the banquet of grace, that is, the eucharist. The celebration of Mass in which the word is heard and the eucharist is offered and received forms but one single act of divine worship.[7]

The unity of the two elements (word-sacrament; Liturgy of the Word and Liturgy of the Eucharist) causes us to stop and wonder at a new phenomenon that is happening in the Roman Catholic Church today: namely, Sunday celebrations of the Word without the Mass. Sometimes people will say to me, "Isn't it wonderful that laity are leading Sunday services and giving out Communion in Brazil," and I will answer, "No, I think it is tragic!" I respond that way, not because I am against lay involvement; not because they are receiving Communion; but rather because they are *not* celebrating the Eucharist. They are being denied their baptismally given right to Eucharistize.

To receive Communion is not the same thing as to celebrate the Eucharist. For example, what we do on Good Friday (a Communion service) is a totally different thing from what we do on Holy Saturday night or every Sunday at Mass. The Mass, the Eucharist, is an action, not a thing. The medieval missals stated: *Hic incipit canonis actio missae.*

We must not lose sight of the venerable fact that the Mass is an *actio*, and an action of *all* those gathered together, priest and people, not just the priest. Under the leadership of the priest-celebrant we all celebrate the Mass. The Mass is not the priest's Mass, it is our Mass, and it is an *actio*. "We come to you, Father, with praise and thanksgiving, through Jesus Christ your Son," as it has been expressed down through the centuries in the Roman Canon.

Receiving a previously consecrated host is a fine thing, but it is not what celebrating the Eucharist is about. My fear is that we will eventually have a generation of Catholics who will have lost sight of the difference. Ordained priests will travel about, consecrating and filling tabernacles with hosts to be given out at services of the Word, even on Sundays. If this is done long enough, our people will get used to it, and not even realize that they have been denied their right to celebrate the Eucharist.

The *Ordo Lectionum Missae* stated: "It can never be forgotten, therefore, that the divine word read and proclaimed by the Church in the liturgy has as its goal the sacrifice of the New Covenant and the banquet of grace, that is, the eucharist." That must be understood in the fullest sense, that is, of the celebration of the Mass, not of a Communion service. We can ask ourselves if a shortage of priests today is not causing the frustration of the logical completion of the Word resolving itself in sacrament. The Word itself cries out for completion, for fulfillment that is achieved only in the Eucharist. I, for one, pray for a solution to the problem, and dream of the day when every local group of Christians can gather on Sundays not just to hear the Word and receive Communion, but to hear the Word proclaimed, and let that Spirit-filled Word lead to the Spirit-filled *action* of celebrating the Eucharist.

The Spirit and the Scriptures

The goal of the Eucharist is unity: to gather into one all the members of the Body of Christ and make them one with the Head of that Body, who is Jesus seated at the right hand of the Father, ever living to make intercession for us. That unity is accomplished in and through the Spirit. The Spirit is the principle of unity.

That unity began at our baptism. At that moment we were anointed with the Spirit, just as Jesus was at his baptism. In Acts 10:37-38 we read the account of Peter's preaching the Spirit-filled Word in the house of Cornelius: "The word which was proclaimed throughout all Judea, beginning from Galilee after the baptism which John preached: how God anointed Jesus of Nazareth with the Holy Spirit and with power; how he went about doing good and healing all that were oppressed of the devil, for God was with him." Jesus was anointed with the Spirit, and so are his followers. Through the sacraments of initiation we become the anointed ones of Christ, anointed with the Spirit. Catholics sometimes forget this point and view the priest as the only "anointed one." They forget that the sacrament of order exists only to serve the sacraments of initiation. The priesthood of the ordained is not over and against, or outside of, the priesthood of all believers. It is part of it and stands in relation to it as the part serving the whole. Among those sharing in the priesthood of Christ through Christian initiation, some are ordained to ministries of special service. All, laity and clergy alike, are called to election and holiness. All are "a chosen race, a royal priesthood, a holy nation, God's own people" (1 Peter 2:9). All are anointed with the Spirit.

This life in the Spirit is the journey of the Christian life. The Spirit, given initially in baptism, speaks to us and guides us at every turn of the journey. The Spirit speaks in a *special* way through the Word; indeed, the Word molds us as a potter shapes the clay.

The Spirit speaks to us and guides us in our private reading and praying of the Scriptures, but this process takes on a special prominence when we gather together for prayer. Paragraph 24 of the Constitution on the Sacred Liturgy states:

> Sacred Scripture is of the greatest importance in the celebration of the liturgy. For it is from Scripture that the readings are given and explained in the homily and that psalms are sung; the prayers, collects, and liturgical songs are scriptural in their inspiration; it is from the Scriptures that actions and signs in the liturgy derive their meaning.

Twenty-two years after the Constitution on Sacred Liturgy, we see that the liturgical songs that are scriptural in their inspiration are the ones that are lasting.

Traditionally there have been two objections levied against the Roman collects: they were too intellectual, and they were not sufficiently scriptural. Hopefully, the post-Vatican II revisions of the collects have at least begun to remedy those problems.

"It is from the Scriptures that actions and signs in the liturgy derive their meaning" (CSL, paragraph 24). In the history of liturgy this fact can be seen in a very striking way from the preeminence given to the liturgical book which contained the Scripture readings, the lectionary. When one studies liturgical manuscripts and books (sacramentaries, ordinals, pontificals, rituals, etc.), the lectionary stands out as something very special, and this for three reasons: (1) because of the quality of the parchment used; (2) because of the beautiful illuminations; and (3) because of the remarkable covers on the books. Granted the importance of the visual (the non-verbal), this said a great deal and helped form the liturgical mindset of the early and medieval Christian mind. The Word was truly something very special, something very important.

The Christian mind was molded by the choice of readings. A striking example would be the Lenten Sunday gospel readings in Rome during the fourth century. Due to the scholarly research of Antoine Chavasse, we know that preparation for Easter was dominated at that early period by readings from John's Gospel.[8] There were only three Sundays of Lent and the readings were all from John: John 4 (the woman of Samaria), John 9 (the man born blind), and John 11 (the raising of Lazarus). They gave the three themes of water, light, and life: water (the woman at the well), light (the man born blind), and life (the raising of Lazarus). Each of the three readings is coupled with a reading from the Old Testament, designed to place the gospel story in the framework of salvation history. Fortunately, these key readings have been restored in the recent reform to the heart of Lent, that is, to the third, fourth, and fifth Sundays of Lent. Their traditional themes of water, light, and life work in brilliantly with Lenten catechesis.

In the ancient Church, when the catechumens would have departed after these gospels were proclaimed (and in today's Church where that practice is still maintained), the catechumens would have longed for the day when they could partake fully of the mystery described by these themes of water, light, and life. They would have longed for the day when they could join the baptized to celebrate the Eucharist and partake of the Body and Blood of the Lord.

Those Johannine readings of Lent are a positive example of how the Christian mind can be molded by the choice of readings and how the readings shape our liturgy. The readings can also serve to challenge and bring to task our liturgy when it is not what it should be. Let me give an example. During the early Middle Ages, as the Gelasian Sacramentary shows, there were three Masses provided for Holy Thursday: a Mass for the reconciliation of penitents, the chrism Mass, and an evening Mass commemorating the Last Supper.[9] This practice probably represents that of the parish churches of Rome. But early in the seventh century, the papal practice at the Lateran knew only one Mass on Holy Thursday, and during this Mass the pope blessed the chrism.

Today there are two Masses provided: the chrism Mass and the Mass of the Lord's Supper. The chrism Mass can be held on an earlier day if there is difficulty in gathering the assembly on Holy Thursday morning. The traditional focus of this liturgy has always been the blessing of the oils and the consecration of the chrism, with the chrism holding primacy of place. Pope Paul VI added something totally new: the "Renewal of Commitment to Priestly Service" to take place after the homily. The danger in this addition is that it risks throwing attention off the chrism and putting undue emphasis on the ordained priesthood to the detriment of the priesthood of all believers. In other words, it runs the risk of clericalizing the chrism Mass.[10] Granted that chrism is used as part of the liturgy of ordination of priests and bishops; nevertheless, the primary symbolism of chrism pertains to Christian initiation, to becoming a Christian.

J. Frank Henderson, rightly points out that the risk of clericalizing the chrism Mass begins with the very opening prayer, which is worded: "Father, by the power of the Holy Spirit you anointed your only Son Messiah and Lord of creation; you have given us a share in his consecration to priestly service in your Church." Henderson comments: "My question regarding this prayer is, to whom does the 'us' refer? Is it a prayer of the entire eucharistic assembly, or is it a prayer of the ordained priests alone?"[11]

His point is important, as the presidential prayers, although said by the priest celebrant, are pronounced in the name of all. Paragraph 33 of the Constitution on the Sacred Liturgy says: "The prayers addressed to God by the priest, who presides over the assembly in the person of Christ, are said in the name of the entire holy people and of all present."

This clericalization of the chrism Mass is challenged by the readings themselves. The first reading from Deutero-Isaiah speaks basically of the total salvation of God's people, and the second reading from the Book of Revelation reminds us that we have been freed from our sins by the Blood of Christ and have been made "a royal nation of priests in the service of his God and Father" (Isa 61:1-3, 6, 8-9; Rev 1:5-8).

So, if paragraph 24 of the Constitution on the Sacred Liturgy states that "the prayers, collects, and liturgical songs are scriptural in their inspiration," how are we to judge the opening collect of this chrism Mass? From this example we see that the Word of God not only forms and shapes our liturgical piety; at times it stands in judgment of it.

Implication for Celebration

I have been stressing the interconnection between Word and sacrament. The principle of this connection is the very Spirit of God, thus my title, "Spirit Through Word." An important element in this Liturgy of the Word is the homily. It plays a key role in this link between Word and sacrament. The *Praenotanda* of the *Ordo Lectionum* puts it well:

> The purpose of the homily at Mass is that the spoken word of God and the liturgy of the eucharist may together become 'a proclamation of God's wonderful works in the history of salvation, the mystery of Christ.' Through the readings and homily Christ's paschal mystery is proclaimed; through the sacrifice of the Mass it becomes present (paragraph 24).

A homilist is a bridge-builder. The task of the homily is to apply the paschal mystery to the particular assembled community. That means the homilist must be a person of faith, a person of the Word; a person who knows the paschal mystery, but also a person who knows *this* congregation.

We are at this point, at least in my opinion, at the heart of a major problem. We have many homilists who know the Paschal Mystery, but who do not know the community to whom they are preaching. It is imperative that ministers come to know their communities. This is not always easy. It takes a long time to get to know the heartbeat of a community, and it must be learned from "within," not from "without." The process of getting to know the local community can be made even longer due to the type of training and life-style that candidates for ministry receive in our seminaries. We have set up a system that separates them for years from the very communities they are meant to serve. After leaving the seminaries, many newly ordained priests have to be "deprogrammed" by living in the midst of their people. Some, unfortunately, always stay in a world "apart." Then, in spite of their prayerfulness, in spite of their grasp of the paschal mystery, they can never truly preach, they can never bridge that gap between the mystery of God in his Word, and that mystery lived out in the flesh and blood lives of Christian women and men.

Having seen the connection between Word and sacrament from the point of view of the homily, let us briefly view that same connection by the example of the Communion antiphon, which has frequently served as a bridge between the gospel and the Communion rite. A key line or phrase from the gospel is repeated, now to be understood in the light of what has transpired, namely, the celebration of the Eucharist. The Prodigal Son liturgy of the second Saturday of Lent is a good example. Interpreted in the Eucharistic context, new meaning is attached to: "Rejoice, because your brother who was dead now lives." We must not give up that connection between Word and sacrament by substituting just any old hymn to replace the Communion antiphon.

From all that we have been saying, we see that the relationship between Word and sacrament can best be understood from the role of the Spirit. It is through the Word that the community gathers together in the Spirit. The Spirit brings about the Eucharistic mystery: through sharing in the one bread and one cup all are formed by the Spirit into the one Body of Christ. This action is accomplished in the context of faith, which faith springs from the Word and expresses itself in the Word.

We have seen how by its very nature, the Word brings us to the action of the Eucharist. We have seen how the Word is itself a thanksgiving, a memorial, and even an *epiclesis*. "Spirit through Word" is even a good description of the Christian life. But it is an even better description of the Christian liturgy, where the Spirit gathers together into the one Body of Christ men and women of every age, race, and temperament.

Let me now say a few words about the ecumenical lectionary, the Common Lectionary. The 1981 *Ordo Lectionum* provided for adaptations and translation. Paragraph 112 stated:

> The lectionary for Mass must be translated integrally in all its parts, including the Introduction. If the conference of bishops has judged it necessary and useful to add certain adaptations, these are to be incorporated after their confirmation by the Holy See.

Thus the matter of adaptation was once again underscored.

A major ecumenical move in our day has been the widespread adoption of the Roman Lectionary by many of the English-speaking Protestant communions. Our dreams of the same lessons being proclaimed in Christian Churches, and joint ecumenical effort in homily preparations are finally being realized. In the process of refining all this, the (North American) Consultation on Common Texts (CCT) convened a meeting in 1978 of all the Churches using the Roman Lectionary. A good summary by Horace Allen appeared in the *FDLC Newsletter* (March–April 1985). The result of the meeting was the establishment of a working group that produced the *Common Lectionary: The Lectionary Proposed by the Consultation on Common Texts.* [12]

The gospel pericopes for all three years are retained with no significant changes. The same is true for the second lessons. The real changes take place for the first readings, especially the use of the Hebrew Bible readings for the Sundays after Pentecost. The basic difference from the Roman Lectionary is that the Common Lectionary uses the first reading in a semi-continuous way rather than having it be hooked up with the gospel as is done in the Roman Lectionary. In my opinion, the Common Lectionary represents a laudable effort to use well the Hebrew Bible in our liturgy and to confront problems of typology. The Common Lectionary has been proposed for use on a trial basis until the end of 1986.

Our American bishops voted overwhelmingly in their November 1982 meeting for an experimental use of that Common Lectionary, but the final approval to do so has not yet been received from Rome. From my own ecumenical experience in recent years, I pray that we American Roman Catholics can take part in this common ecumenical Christian venture. I see the Spirit operating today in the United States among Christians of different denominations. Granted the closely-knit and open system operative in our country, I do not think we Roman Catholics should stand outside such important ecumenical ventures. Without being overly dramatic about it, our topic has special pertinence to this whole question of our sharing the use of the Common Lectionary: "Spirit Through Word." It is even more to the point in that we have been viewing Word as leading to sacrament, the Liturgy of the Word as ordered to the Liturgy of the Eucharist, where the Spirit gathers into one all the members of the Body of Christ! Our ecumenical journey must begin with the Word of God, and hopefully it will be led by the Spirit to one day share in the sacrament of unity, when all Christian Churches will meet in common Eucharist.

Let me bring this to a conclusion. You are important people, doing important work in the Church. You are people concerned with liturgical spirituality: with faith shaping prayer, and prayer shaping faith.

In preparing this lecture I used Yves Congar's masterful three-volume work *I Believe in the Holy Spirit.* I was very touched by the title of his very last chapter, "The Life of the Church as One Long Epiclesis."[13] May your liturgical apostolates begin in and through the Word, and lead to a Spirit-filled life!

Let me tie that in with one final quote from the *Praenotanda* of the *Ordo Lectionum* (paragraph 9):

> The working of the Holy Spirit is needed if the word of God is to make what we hear outwardly have its effect inwardly. Because of the Holy Spirit's inspiration and support, the word of God becomes the foundation of the liturgical celebration and the rule and support of all our life. May that same Holy Spirit be the foundation of your liturgical work, and may your own personal journey be led by that Spirit through the Word of God into a unity that will never end!

Notes

1. See, for example, Gregory Dix, *The Shape of the Liturgy* (London: Dacre Press, 1964) 36–47.

2. A. M. Roguet, "The Whole Mass Proclaims the Word of God," in *The Liturgy and the Word of God* (Collegeville: The Liturgical Press, 1959) 72.

3. Aidan Kavanagh, *The Shape of Baptism: The Rite of Christian Initiation* (New York: Pueblo Publishing Company, 1978) 25.

4. Roguet, "The Whole Mass Proclaims the Word of God" 72.

5. See Louis Bouyer, *Eucharist: Theology and Spirituality of the Eucharistic Prayer* (Notre Dame: University of Notre Dame Press, 1968) 33.

6. See Yves M. J. Congar, *I Believe in the Holy Spirit*, vol. 1 (New York: Seabury Press, 1983) 12.

7. Translation is taken from: Liturgy Documentary Series, no. 1, *Lectionary for Mass: Introduction.* Washington: United States Catholic Conference, 1982.

8. See Thierry Maertens, "History and Function of the Three Great Pericopes," in Johannes Wagner, ed., *Adult Baptism and the Catechumenate,* Concilium vol. 22 (New York: Paulist Press, 1967) 51–56.

9. L. C. Mohlberg, ed., *Liber Sacramentorum Romanae Aeclesiae Ordinis Anni Circuli* (Rome: Herder, 1960) 55–64.

10. See Niels Rasmussen, "The Chrism Mass: Tradition and Renewal," in *The Cathedral: A Reader* (Washington: United States Catholic Conference Publications, 1979) 29–33.

11. J. Frank Henderson, "The Chrism Mass of Holy Thursday," *Worship* 51 (1977) 150.

12. Published by The Church Hymnal Corporation, 800 Broad Ave., New York, New York, 10017.

13. See Yves M. J. Congar, *I Believe in the Holy Spirit*, vol. 3 (New York: Seabury Press, 1983) 267–74.

2

Sacraments: For the Peace and Salvation of All the World

THERESA F. KOERNKE, I.H.M.

*T*he overall theme of this gathering, "Liturgy and Spirituality," would have been a simply marvelous topic ten or fifteen years ago. Today, I find myself wanting to slowly step backward, turn, and run. Syllabi and workshop brochures feature opportunities to discover Ignatian, Franciscan, holistic and creation, ecological and Eastern spirituality, to name a few. Then, of course, there is liturgical spirituality. I am regularly reminded that there are diverse "styles" of spirituality. Some people are "into" liturgy, others are not, and who is anyone to say that the public worship of the Church is central to Christian spiritual life? That just isn't where some people are, I am assured. They don't prefer it. When recently asked to address the topic of liturgical spirituality, Aidan Kavanagh felt like a horse in a burning barn.[1] Now I know why!

It seems clear that the descendants of Ignatius, Francis, Theresa, and Alphonsus can be recognized, but unless I am sorely mistaken, these giants would be horrified at what has at times become a supermarket scenario: as if the object of Christian life is to find a spirituality, or as if the object of liturgical prayer is to find a style and a spirituality that fits our preferences.

Hence, there are several possible subtitles for this presentation, one of which is "A Modest Proposal for Avoiding the Domestication of the Church." For I can't help but wonder whether what passes for renewed, pastorally sensitive liturgy may not really be the domestication of the one liturgy of the Christ and his Body for the peace and salvation of all the world. Regis Duffy has captured the concern in his work *Real Presence: Worship, Sacraments, and Commitment:* "Why is there so much worship and so little commitment?"[2] Quite simply, the meaning of liturgical spirituality, if there be such, can take its place within the answer to that question.

Before getting into the body of my reflections, I would share with you some musings on assumptions, for the issue of operative assumptions is crucial and not at all new.

Perhaps the greatest paradox in the nineteen-hundred-year history of the Church is the actual, conceptual separation between what we think we are doing in our daily societal actions and what we think we are doing in our public liturgy, especially the Eucharist, the memorial of the Lord.

In a volume entitled *Documents on the Liturgy, 1963–1979,** the International Commission on English in the Liturgy has gathered every conciliar, papal and curial text on the liturgy, beginning with the Constitution on the Sacred Liturgy, promulgated in 1963 by the Second Vatican Council.

In perusing the general index of that mammoth vol-

*published by The Liturgical Press, Collegeville, Minnesota, 1983 ume, one finds no entries under justice, social justice, social activity, or related topics. Under the entry "sin/social consequences," there are three indirect references: the first to the penitential nature of Lent (SSC, 109), the second to the fact that sin affects the social bond within the Church (audience of Paul VI, March 12, 1973), and the third, a very abstruse reference within a caution against the use of general absolution (reply to USA, SC Doctrine of the Faith, January 20, 1978).

Now then, it may be unfair to critique authors for not doing what you would have liked them to do. So, let me simply and honestly ask: Is it not at least interesting that in the major liturgical document of that great council, there is no extended discussion of the relation between what we do in our daily social activities and what we do when we gather to remember the Lord?

I am aware that there are, indeed, a myriad of statements in other documents regarding the mission of the Church, about the relation of the Church to the world, and surely we are familiar with the opening paragraph of The Constitution on the Church in the Modern World:

> The joys and the hopes, the griefs and anxieties of the men and women of this age, especially those who are poor and in any way afflicted, these too are the joys and hopes, the griefs and anxieties, of the followers of Christ.

And, even though the Constitution on the Sacred Liturgy enunciated the importance of liturgical reform for the renewal of Church life, is it not at least interesting that this document never explicitly returns to the crucial connection between liturgical worship and the social life of the faithful? In an ecclesial community so identified by its liturgical/sacramental life, is it not at least interesting that in a document which asserts that "the liturgy is the source and summit of Christian life," (SSC 10) that no explicit discussion is given to its relation to societal right-relations, and in a document which asserts that this ecclesial community is in the world to serve it (The Constitution on the Church in the Modern World), that there is no explicit discussion of what its liturgical activity has to do with that societal project?

Perhaps the greatest irony in the nineteen-hundred-year history of the Church is the separation between what we assume we are doing in our daily social activities and what we assume we are doing when we gather to remember the Lord.

It is true that the elements of a theology of social responsibility rooted in Eucharistic faith are scattered about the documents of the Second Vatican Council. But the overall statement of the council, I would submit, reflected a fact of life: "The failure of Christian people and Christian leaders to acknowledge the essential connection between liturgy and society, . . ."[3] that is, the essential connection between worship and living morally, between worship and the peace and salvation of all the world.

Why? What are the operative, unspoken assumptions,[4] in the minds and hearts of Catholics, which have permitted this separation? Again, the issue of operative assumptions is crucial and not at all new. What did certain Corinthians (1 Cor 10-11) assume about "being in Christ," about recognizing the Body of Christ, that allowed them to eat and drink in the presence of the poor, and thereafter to presume to celebrate the Eucharist? How could a culture known for its cathedrals, monasteries, and universities have given rise to the savagery of the Holocaust? How could so many of the other nations of Europe have been so willing to cooperate? Why have the worst racial conflicts in this country obtained in the most densely Catholic cities: New York, Boston, Detroit, Chicago, Los

Angeles? What could be going on in the heads and hearts of Catholics who question the very right of bishops to address the global, societal issues of nuclear war and the economy? Indeed, both in Europe and on this continent, social action and liturgical renewal have run parallel tracks, occasionally meeting in people like Fr. H. A. Reinhold, Dorothy Day, and Virgil Michel, but more often than not, disparaging each other. So we have heard: "Why get so upset about what goes on in church? Forget it! Get out where the action is!" Or: "The Liturgy is the most important thing we do! There we receive the Lord and the strength to apply his love to the world."

I would flatly submit that both of these comments may sound good at first blush. But they reflect the very operative assumption which has run social action and the renewal of the worship of the Church on parallel tracks. And, dare I suggest, that that operative assumption has led either to a refusal to implement liturgical reform or to the submission of public worship to the demands of a therapy session, or to the success criteria of Madison Avenue. Some of us have thought we should go where the action is and leave the institutional Church to wallow in its seeming absurdities (as if there are two Churches!). Others have become preoccupied with the liturgy so as to turn it into yet another aesthetic play—thing. Some of us have imagined that we have made the liturgy relevant by sitting around coffee tables, or by aping the format of the Johnny Carson Show, or by strictly forbidding the presence of men, or by passing the Sacramentary around during the Eucharistic Prayer "to make the folks feel involved." Need I mention the playing of anti-war songs during the entrance procession and the presentation of footballs, cleats, and pom-poms at the Offertory? Still others yearn for the seemingly euphoric quicksand of the Tridentine Rite. But I wonder if these behaviors cannot be compared, as Mark Searle has pointed out, to the effects of a low-level earth tremor. To relate the post-Vatican II situation to Einstein's comments about nuclear fission: "Everything has changed but the way we think."

In his work *The Making of Disciples,* Enda McDonagh asserts "the duty of moral theologians to explore the relationship between liturgy and morality," and states that the articulation of this relation is for the most part incomplete.[5] The following is a small contribution, by a liturgical theologian, to explore the relationship between liturgy and moral theology, that is, between liturgy and the peace and salvation of all the world.

Whereas we do well to caution against a reductionism which equates worship with service in the world,[6] we do well to recognize them as "isomorphic." Webster reads "isomorph: something identical with or similar to something else in form or structure." Straightforwardly, then, worship and living morally share the same form or structure. Indeed, New Testament texts refer to Zechariah's service in the Temple (Luke 1:23), to collection of money for the missions (2 Cor 9:12), to Epaphroditus' fellowship with Paul (Phil 2:30), and to the total response of the Christ in worship of the Father (Heb 8:6) by the one word *leitourgia.* The New Testament, then, insists that Christian worship is spiritual and bodily. It insists that the activity of faith is in the first place not assent to that which is outside one, but the response of one's entire being in witness to the Gospel, in serving the needs of others, and in private and communal prayer.[7]

The author of the Fourth Gospel provides an explanation of the basic trait of all Christian worship. It cannot be limited to or equated with any geographical place—neither the Samaritan Mount Gerizim nor Jerusalem (4:21), nor even primarily in the interior of the human spirit. [8] Indeed, worship is possible only in the embrace of the Spirit of God . . . the Spirit, bestowed by the crucified-risen Lord from the Father, who reveals the truth about our God. It is that Spirit who teaches us all we need to know. It is that Spirit by whom we are baptized, drawn into the justice of God. What, then, is so important about the proper celebration of the public, communal worship of the Church? Why ought we be concerned about playing with the rites?

To respond to this question, we consider the following: (1) Baptism in Paul, (2) Memory of the Heart and Discipleship, (3) "Do this in memory of me."

Baptism in Paul

In Romans 6 Paul is not commenting on the liturgical rite of baptism, but on the reality of faith: the union of the Christian with Christ, and of the incorporation of the believer into the Body of Christ, the living congregation of those bound to the Lord in the New Covenant. [9] The setting is "the contrast of the two dominions and their lords." Paul's concern is to answer certain objections which might arise to the thesis of justification by grace through faith *in Christ* which he has argued in chapters 1–5.

> What shall we say then? Are we to continue in sin that grace may abound? By no means! How can we who died to sin still be alive in it? (6:1-2)

Paul's interest, then, is in the decisive transfer of the believer from the dominion of sin to the dominion of grace (v. 6). As such, believers may and must walk in the new life (v. 9) as a present participation in the life of what will be in their future resurrection through dying with Christ (v. 3). Paul refers to baptism, even though it is beside his immediate point here, because he assumes that the idea of dying with Christ in baptism is known and accepted. The genuine understanding of it grounds his argument and the ability of his hearers to understand that, even though the old dominion (order) continues to exist and to exert its power, their being in Christ, always and everywhere, is the source of overcoming that power and of living morally, of living for God in Christ.[10]

In speaking of baptism, then, we are speaking primarily of the reality of faith, of our being drawn into, plunged, grafted into the death of the Lord for the hope of resurrection. This is the reality, the activity, the response to God in which we have our being together. In speaking of baptism, we are speaking of entrance into the fundamental orientation of God to the world and of a fundamental orientation of humanity to God, which by its very nature implies a complex of relations and spirituality.

To some spirituality suggests a kind of hot-house atmosphere in which people are unduly preoccupied with their own inward condition to the neglect of social responsibility. However, in spite of all misunderstandings, no amount of distortion can ever destroy the fact that, fundamentally, Christian spirituality has to do with our response to our Father, *in Christ*, through the Spirit.[11] A response, not in Buddha or in Ghandi, Ignatius, or Francis, as magnificent as their lives may have been, but *in the Christ*, and him crucified.

Universally, we may speak of spirituality as a phenomenon, the internal and external response to one's experience of the Absolute by whatever name. It is the result of the experience of relationship with and distinction from the Nameless One. Further, one's spirituality is conditioned by the fact of one's identity, by all the factors which contribute to that identity, above all by one's human relationships. The point: there is no purely individual or private experience of the Holy, but always, that experience as mediated.[12]

How is this universal phenomenon specified by the Christian experience of God, that is, by our plunge into Christ's dying: a scandal to those who seek marvelous signs, and foolishness to those who are seeking earthly wisdom (1 Cor 1:22)?

Christian spirituality is the internal and external response to one's experience of the Absolute as revealed in the life, death, and resurrection of the Christ. It is the result of the experience of relationship with and of distinction from the no longer Nameless One, but of our Father-Mother. Further, Christian spirituality is conditioned by the fact of one's identity, by all the factors, glorious and wretched, which contribute to one's identity, above all by the experience of human relationships, glorious and wretched, in the Church. The "Catholic thing," as Rosemary Haughton has so delightfully pointed out, is radically earthy, rootedly communal.[13]

However, in the highly individualistic society in which we live, community is such a multivalent term. Sometimes it means a neighborhood, or an ethnic group, or even a religious congregation. More often than not, it carries a sense of the ideal, expressed in comments like "we should work at building community," or "there was such a feeling of community at that liturgy." In this sense we all have our own vision of what makes community, and measuring sticks for its existence.[14] Yet Dietrich Bonhoeffer cautioned against confusing the ecclesial community of which Paul speaks with "feelings of conviviality." He warned:[15]

> Just at this point Christian brotherhood is threatened most often at the very start by the greatest danger of all, the danger of being poisoned at its root, the danger of confusing Christian brotherhood with the wishful idea of religious fellowship,

of confounding the natural desire of the devout heart for community with the spiritual reality of Christian brotherhood. In Christian brotherhood everything depends upon its being clear from the beginning, first, that Christian brotherhood is not an ideal, but a divine reality, Second, that Christian brotherhood is not . . . a psychic reality.

Quite simply, the experience of Christian community is not primarily a matter of "feeling convivial." The *ekklesia* of which Paul speaks is already given, it is The Given, not something to be worked for, but recognized even when we do not feel it. This *ekklesia* is the gathering of, the calling together of disciples into our God's embrace of the world in Christ. This embrace is what disciples remember. It has little to do with conviviality, and everything to do with the Cross.

Memory of the Heart and Discipleship

Perhaps one of the richest results of biblical scholarship for contemporary theology has been the retrieval of the notion of discipleship, and so, of the *ekklesia* as the gathering of disciples. [16] The Greek word *mathitis* simply means pupil, follower, one who is taught. The Church, then, is the community of those who, having been taught or disciplined by the Lord, remember in the following.

Now, it seems clear that the disciples of Jesus did not all-at-once understand the full impact of his teaching. Recall the Emmaus story in Luke 24. It was only after his death that they came to knowledge of his identity, and to knowledge of the cost of discipleship.

Each of us, like the disciples on the Emmaus Road, has been confused, and has asked: What shall we do? How shall we know what is good? To whom shall we go to be taught? And in Luke we find an exquisite statement of the faith of the Church that in the Breaking of the Bread, we come to know what is good, we come to know what to do, and we recognize the One who teaches us. Knowledge, as I use it here, is not information, but primarily that pre-conceptual knowledge of the heart, the experience of the Spirit who is the memory of our hearts.

As a child I used to wish I could rush up alongside that young man in the Gospels and ask: "Teacher, what good deed must I do to have eternal life?" (Matt 19:16-22 and parallels). And I suspect we have each been tempted to think that if we could see and touch and hear the Lord, our problems would be solved . . . until we read that even though that lucky man could ask, "What must I do?", right there in the flesh, and hear the answer, "Go, sell what you have and follow me," he turned away, for he had many idols.

All this is to say that those who could physically see and touch and hear the Teacher have no corner on access to him. For it is the *Consolation of the Faith* that this community of disciples, here, for all of its weaknesses, has for its most intimate Gift *The Spirit Who Binds Us Together*, who disposes our hearts to be taught, who teaches us all we need to know, who enables us to remember what we must do.

Recently, Richard McCormick stated that specific action guides are not the only glue of a community. Indeed, a community will not exist for long unless it is glued together around shared convictions that affect action and policies of behavior.[17] What convictions? Conviction that what has transpired in the flesh of Jesus of Nazareth is the basis of our hope as well (Rom 6:5); that the Teacher can never be separated from the disciples (Rom 8:31-39); that the disciples live and move and have their being in the Teacher (Eph 1:3-14); that if the Teacher is crucified, so are the disciples (John 15:18ff.). So, discipleship involves far more than leafing through the Scriptures to come up with an ethical code, a set of specific action guides. Discipleship primarily involves the acknowledgment that we are continually being taught by the Lord in whom we have our being in the embrace of the Spirit. Our Law is the Spirit who teaches us to remember, not only specific action guides, but to remember the Holy One in whose response to God we dwell.

If that be our faith, what does it mean for this *ekklesia* of disciples to gather and remember? To be sure, human beings have the faculty of memory, the aptitude to register and conserve events and words which affectively mark their personalities. But the memory to which I refer is the inexhaustible living ground of all our acts of intellect and will, the profound memory, the memory of the heart which engenders the desire for God, by whatever Name. It pertains to the order of the movement of the whole being toward God, and for those drawn into the dying and rising of the Lord, the Spirit of the Lord may be called "the living memory of the heart." In this sense the Spirit continually calls disciples to place themselves on the way of faith, that is, within the response to God in which they exist, Christ crucified and risen.[18] It is the Spirit who, as John says, goads the heart, who enables us to come to conclusions of which rational logic knows little, who continually calls disciples, those disciplined by the Lord, to know with Paul: It is no longer I who live but Christ lives in me, and that putting on Christ is done at the cost of one's life.

This understanding of the Spirit as living memory of the heart, and therefore as the living memory of the *ekklesia* of disciples, is at the root of what we do in *anamnesis*, in making memory of the Lord. To be sure, we hold that the Spirit is active in all creation, present to every human being. But for the disciples of the Lord, the Spirit is concretely, personally revealed in the flesh of Jesus of

Nazareth. For those grafted into the Lord, the Spirit not only hands on the tradition about Jesus, i.e., specific words and events, but hands on the Lord himself. [19] Hence, when the *ekklesia* at the Eucharist proclaims, "Calling to mind the death your Son endured for our salvation," it is not only registering a past event, but opening itself to the memory of its heart, opening itself to the Spirit who has bound it to the crucified Teacher in baptism, and from whom it can never be separated.

"Do this in memory of me."

What does making memory of the Lord mean, then, for disciples, for those who live in the Crucified One? What is the relationship between the cross and the meal? What is the antecedent of the pronoun "this" in the Lord's command, "Do this in memory of me"?

Christians have pointed to the cross as the fullest statement of the initiative of God, the most shocking and joyful statement of God to human beings. Indeed, the liturgy of Good Friday sings hymns to the cross, and in the Great Vigil, the Exultet exhorts the very earth to rejoice because of the Cross.

The Epistle to the Hebrews is an extended commentary on the cross, the ultimate self-gift of Jesus to the Father in the eternal Spirit. There we read that in the eternal Spirit, Jesus in his flesh, enters into the eternal sanctuary, making our peace with God (Heb 9–10). His self-offering is the perfect moral, i.e., human, act, the perfect act of worship of our God in the Spirit. On the cross, then, is revealed the normative relation of our Mother-Father God to human beings, of human beings to our God, of human beings among themselves . . . a scandal to those seeking marvelous signs and foolishness to those seeking earthly wisdom.

Using the principle of analogy, more contemporary theologians have examined the love between persons[20] as a way of getting some deeper insight into why disciples do well to rejoice in the cross. By using this analogy we can see that in the union of genuine love persons allow full amplitude to each other, to be who they each are. The bond of love does not efface differences. In genuine love the otherness and difference of each person grow in the manner in which their unity grows in depth. Thus, the locus of any understanding of God's relation to the world is the love between persons.

In his life and cross the love between Jesus and Abba is indefectible, so our God permits Jesus to be fully human, to assume the form of sinner, a being radically different from God, and to experience the consequences of what is utterly not God, sin and death. Love does not efface differences. But the love between Jesus and Abba is indefectible. The Spirit by which Jesus and Abba love each other makes it unfitting that death should hold him. Love is stronger than death.

In this life and cross it is revealed that our God is radically related to us, is indefectibly in love with the world. And there too it is revealed that by abandoning oneself to the love between our God and Jesus, i.e., by abandoning oneself to the memory of our hearts, one comes to the highest degree of understanding of one's creaturehood and of one's freedom. Such abandonment is perfect worship, the perfect moral act. And if it is in the embrace of the indefectible Spirit that the Incarnate Word is able to offer perfect worship, and if it is that same Spirit whom Jesus has bestowed upon his disciples from the cross, then we get some deeper insight into Paul's proclamation: By the one Spirit you have been grafted, inserted into the death of the Lord for the hope of resurrection. We dare to say:

By the one Spirit we have been grafted, inserted into the perfect relational activity, the perfect activity of love, of faith, of worship and obedience, into the justice of God.

Bearing this in mind, we have some better insight into the antecedent of the pronoun "this" in the Lord's command: "Do this in memory of me."

In Eucharistic Prayer III we pray:

Father . . . .

On the night he was betrayed,
he took bread and gave you thanks and praise.
He broke the bread, gave it to his disciples, and said:
Take this, all of you, and eat it:
this is my body which will be given up for you.

When supper was ended, he took the cup.
Again he gave you thanks and praise,
gave the cup to his disciples, and said:

Take this, all of you, and drink from it:
this is the cup of my blood,
the blood of the new and everlasting covenant.
It will be shed for you and for all
so that sins may be forgiven.
Do this in memory of me. . . .

Father, calling to mind the death your Son endured for our
    salvation,
his glorious resurrection and ascension into heaven,
and ready to greet him when he comes again,
we offer you in thanksgiving this holy and living sacrifice.

Look with favor on your Church's offering,
and see the Victim whose death has reconciled us to yourself.
Grant that we, who are nourished by his body and blood,
may be filled with his Holy Spirit,
and become one body, one spirit in Christ.

May he make us an everlasting gift to you
and enable us to share in the inheritance of your saints . . . .

Lord, may this sacrifice,
which has made our peace with you,
advance the peace and salvation of all the world. . . .

We hope to enjoy for ever the vision of your glory,
through Christ our Lord, from whom all good things come.
Through him,
with him,
in him,
in the unity of the Holy Spirit,
all glory and honor is yours,
almighty Father,
for ever and ever. [21]

Every New Testament account of the command "Do this" is situated on the night he was betrayed. In the memory of the Church, the meal and the cross make no sense without each other. In its imagination—in that capacity to put things together at which rational logic balks—the Church knows that it draws its life from the Eucharist, for there it makes anamnesis of the death that has reconciled us to God and to each other; there it remembers the death in which it is indefectibly plunged in baptism.

And so, precisely because of our baptism, we offer the one sacrifice, not another sacrifice, but the one eternal sacrifice of praise in which we live and die. What we are commanded to DO is the Body broken, the Blood poured out, in which we live and move and have our being. In the Eucharist the Lord offers himself to his Body. Do THIS is his command. Do my Body given for you. Do my life poured out for you. Do the justice of God in which you dwell. "Do this in memory of me."

We pray: "Look with favor on your Church's offering, and recognize the Victim whose death has reconciled us to yourself." This prayer is either the crassest of blasphemies or the profoundest statement of the meaning of our mystical union with the crucified-risen Lord. I submit the latter.

In our Eucharist we make grateful remembrance of the self-offering of the Lord in which we live; there we make explicit what is always going on; there we attend formally to that permanent, radical orientation into which we have been plunged and which gives ultimate value to every human activity. There we give free reign to the memory of our hearts . . . at the cost of our lives.

Conclusion

This paper has been about operative assumptions and about the faith of the Church. We have asked serious questions about attitudes which dichotomize worship and life. We have asserted that choosing a spirituality is not the object of Christian life, but that life in Christ by the power of the Spirit to the glory of the Father is, and that Christian life is primarily ecclesial and derivatively individual, or it is an illusion.

In this sense the public worship of the Church is the source of moral knowledge, that is, the source of our corporate knowledge of what is good, of what is the relation of our God to the world, of human beings to each other, of humanity to God in Christ. He is the justice of God, and we live in that justice, in that one liturgy.

Hence, what we do, how we each behave when we gather must be adapted to this justice, this right-relation. With this in mind, I submit a concern about what transpires under the aegis of making the folks feel welcome and making the liturgy relevant.

If one understands, with regard to presbyters, what it means to convene the *ecclesia* of disciples, to call it to attention for the purpose of making memorial of the sacrifice, does it make good sense to say "Hi there" or "Please pray with me" or "Good morning! Wasn't Pete Rose something else last night?" If one understands that the Eucharistic Prayer, proclaimed in the name of the Church, is addressed to the Father, in praise and thanksgiving, in *anamnesis* of the Lord, does it make good sense to reduce the Eucharistic Prayer as a whole to an address to the congregation, and the words of institution to a drama of the Last Supper? (As a teacher once quipped to aspiring seminarians: "You are not Jesus and this is not a play!") If good catechesis and preaching obtain, why would a member of the assembled Church imagine that reading a paragraph from the Sacramentary is what it takes to get involved in what is going on? If we realized what the presbyterate is, why would a bishop pipe up during the presbyteral imposition of hands: "I'll bet you folks would really like to get in on this!" Is there only one charism? And on and on.

Volumes have been written on the importance of ritual in the life of a community. Our behaviors at worship, without anyone's permission, are resounding statements of what we believe. It often is not clear that the activities mentioned above (and others) express the faith of the Church.

As we celebrate the twenty-second anniversary of the promulgation of The Constitution on the Sacred Liturgy, people are dying in a world which the United States could feed. The United States is providing military aid to both sides of any number of conflicts on this planet. Even though international organizations of physicians assure us that we could in no way cope with proper medical treatment, certain leaders chatter on about survival of nuclear conflict. In the face of it all, we simply suggest that the proper celebration of the liturgy in general and of the Eucharist in particular has everything to do with the peace and salvation of this world.

To conclude with the words of Aidan Kavanagh: [22]

No 'spirituality' which runs counter to this [the Cross of the Christ] is worth a Christian's time. No competency which does not master our natural fears over passing this way is worth cultivating. No faith which does not have this at its center is anything but vain. No liturgy which does not celebrate this is anything more than corporate fantasy. No life without this is Christian. And without Christians living this, there is no life in the world. If anyone offers you something other than this as a contemporary, relevant, meaningful, and fulfilling Christian 'spirituality', thank him politely and pour it down the sink.

Notes

1. Aidan Kavanagh, "Spirituality, Really?" *Pastoral Music* 9 (December–January 1985) 17–22.

2. Regis Duffy, *Real Presence: Worship, Sacraments, and Commitment* (San Francisco: Harper and Row, 1982).

3. John J. Egan, *Liturgy and Social Justice: An Unfinished Agenda"* (Collegeville: The Liturgical Press, 1983).

4. For an analysis of the impact of unconscious assumptions upon culture, and hence, upon ritual, ecclesiology and Christology, cf. George Worgul, *From Magic to Metaphor: A Validation of the Christian Sacraments* (New York: Paulist Press, 1980) esp. 3–20.

5. Enda McDonagh, *The Making of Disciples: Tasks of Moral Theology* (Wilmington: Michael Glazier, 1982) 36.

6. William H. Willimon, *The Service of God: Christian Work and Worship* (Nashville: Abingdon Press, 1983) 15.

7. Edward J. Kilmartin, "Communal Worship in the New Testament" *New Catholic World* (March–April 1983) 83.

8. *Ibid.* 84.

9. J. K. Howard, ". . . into Christ: A Study of the Pauline Concept of Baptismal Union," *Expository Times* 79 (1968) 147–50.

10. R. Tannehill, *Dying and Rising With Christ: A Study in Pauline Theology* (Berlin: Topleman, 1967) esp. 7–14.

11. John Macquarrie, "Spirit and Spirituality" in *Paths in Spirituality* (London: SCM Press Ltd., 1972) 40–52.

12. See Karl Rahner, "Reflections of the Unity of the Love of Neighbor and the Love of God," in *Theological Investigations*, vol. VI (New York: Seabury Press, 1974) 231–49.

13. Rosemary Haughton, *The Catholic Thing* (Springfield: Temple-gate Publishers, 1979).

14. Mark Searle, "On the Art of Lifting Up the Heart: Liturgical Prayer Today," *Studies in Formative Spirituality* 3 (1982) 399–410.

15. Dietrich Bonhoeffer, "Community" in *Life Together* (New York: Harper and Row, 1954) esp. 17–39.

16. McDonagh, *The Making of Disciples: Tasks of Moral Theology* esp. 38–59.

17. Richard A. McCormick, "Moral Theological Agenda: An Over-view," *New Catholic World* 226 (1983) 4–7, esp. 7.

18. Jean-Claude Sagne, "La memoir du coeur," *Vie Spirituelle* 132 (1978) 184–99.

19. Walter Kasper and Gerhard Sauter, "Die Kirche als Sakrament des Geistes" in *Kirche—Ort des Geistes.* Kleine Oecumenische Schriften, 18 (Freiburg: Herder, 1976) 13–55.

20. See Medard Kehl and Werner Loeser, "Situation de la Theologie Systematique en Allemagne," *Revue de Theologie et de Philosophie* 112 (1981) 25–38, in which the work of E. Przywara is discussed.

21. From *The Roman Missal* © 1973, 1985, International Committee on English in the Liturgy, Inc.

22. Kavanagh, "Spirituality, Really?" 22.

3

Devotions and Renewal Movements: Spiritual Cousins of the Liturgy

MARY COLLINS, O.S.B.

The framing of the title of this address ("Devotions and Renewal Movements: Spiritual Cousins of the Liturgy") already suggests a formal relationship among the three. The position of the colon makes devotions and renewal movements first cousins, if not siblings, and implies that liturgy is at least once removed, a somewhat distant relative of the preceding pair. In a collaborative intellectual effort, may I ask you to let the colon dissolve and the typography blur? All you have now are the three matters of concern—devotions, renewal movements, liturgy—devoid of any punctuation structuring relationships among them. May I ask you, next, to think about kinship—the reality behind the language of "cousins"—as a simple affirmation of common genesis? Finally, may we agree further that what makes the three spiritual kin is that all arise as expressions of and response to the human experience of God. All three are grounded in mystery, mystery which grasps ordinary people in their ordinary lives and enables them somehow to transcend the mundane.

Let's consider a concrete case. Many popular articles are appearing in the Catholic press on pilgrimages to Yugoslavia, to the site of the reported appearances of the Mother of God to several young Slavs to give them a simple message: "Be brave! Take courage!" The reported presence and message has produced an outcropping of devotion. Hundreds of thousands have made their way to a remote Balkan village, to the dismay of communist and Catholic hierarchy alike. The young visionaries are being heralded as prophets, as those given the gift of speaking God's saving Word in the present situation. In our self-destructive civilization, the words "Be brave! Take courage!" resound as good news, words of hope and comfort. They speak not only to the citizens of Soviet-dominated countries but to all of Western Europe and the whole North Atlantic region as well. Ordinary people are drawn to Medjugorje.

If both Church and State hierarchies are cautious in pronouncing on the authenticity of the messengers in the reported series of events, the people who come to Medjugorje have no doubt about the authenticity of the message. Devotion to Our Lady of Medjugorje flourishes because people are hearing in that place a word which sets them free to trust God, to have hope, and to risk love. The outer word of Medjugorje is touching and stirring the inner word of faith buried deep in the hearts of ordinary people.

Experiences of God are elusive. We catch them only in their refractions—in the images and the attitudes, the words and the deeds to which they give rise. Sometimes the stirrings of the human heart are so fragile, tenuous, elusive, that people might fail to catch them at all if the religiously gifted did not find helpful images to bring experiences of God and longings for God to consciousness. Medjugorje is only one case in point. The point I want to explore with you is this, namely, that devotions, renewal movements, the liturgy—each in its own way—make available to the community of faith the depths of its own existence, its life hidden in God. What we do as Church is fed from inner wellsprings.

Devotion to the Sacred Heart: A Case in Point

Each in its own way. References to an actual case of devotional and liturgical history might best illustrate how each makes its contribution as an expression of faith. Some details of the modern devotion to the Sacred Heart and the liturgical celebration of that event can be reviewed quickly in order to give us a frame within which to talk about the interaction of devotions, renewal movements, and liturgy. My background resources for these observations are the research of Frans Josef van Beeck, Annibale Bugnini, and Raymond Firth, as well as my own. I am indebted to this trio for interpreting the story of the Sacred Heart devotion from their different perspectives as theologian, as liturgical historian, and as cultural anthropologist, but I take responsibility for my own use of their insights.

At the start of his investigation of devotion to the Sacred Heart from the sixteenth through the eighteenth centuries, van Beeck cites the religious historian Peter Brown,

"The quality of a religious system depends perhaps less on its specific doctrine than on the choice of problems that it regards as important, the areas of human experience to which it directs attention."[1]

That observation is pertinent, for it encourages us to consider what choices the Church is making in our day, what problems we regard as important, what human experiences we attend to as Church. Recently, doing a bibliographic search for another project, I discovered that major systematic theologians writing in English have written almost nothing on creation, on sin, and on love in the past decade. Sin, love, and creation are anything but insignificant in our lives as twentieth-century North Americans. In fact, they may be so close to our encounter with mystery that we cannot yet discern spirits and put order into our experiences.

But our first concern in this discussion is history. Whatever the apparent limits of seventeenth- and eighteenth-century Western European spirituality, the Church has always been concerned about love. It is that basic human concern about the mystery of divine and human love which undergirds the rise of devotion to the Sacred Heart of Jesus. Yet, as we suggested earlier, it is artists, poets, saints, visionaries who must find culturally accessible images if ordinary people are to be able to get hold of the mystery of their own inner lives. Devotional images are characteristically colorful, dramatic, flamboyant, extravagant—as they must be to hold our attention. Medjugorje devotees report a "dancing sun," and I have seen photos that certainly demand some explanation.

van Beeck, in a brilliantly suggestive essay, ties the historical development of the modern devotion to the Sacred Heart and its iconography to European cultural history, specifically the history of science and medicine. [2] We know that devotion to the heart of Christ dates back at least to Gertrude the Great of Helfta and her fourteenth-century *Revelations of Divine Love*. But it is only in the sixteenth and seventeenth centuries that the distinctive iconography of the modern devotion appears. What prepared for it was the mid-sixteenth century publication of the first truly modern anatomical atlas. What consolidated the impulse was the early seventeenth-century publication of William Harvey's treatise on the movement of the heart and the circulation of the blood. Certainly there had been earlier, much earlier, devotion to the wounds of Christ, including his lance-pierced side. But anatomical interests in Harvey's "blood-pumping muscle" had dramatically drawn the Christian people's imagination into the dark interior of that wound. An iconographic adventure—the heart of Christ as a scientifically accurate human heart—which began in sixteenth-century Cologne among the Carthusians spread rapidly in a scientifically curious Western European culture. Throughout the seventeenth century this iconography of the human heart invited the devout to contemplate the heart of Jesus in order to discover the truth about their own hearts. Neither theirs nor his were simply blood-pumping muscles; they were burning furnaces of love. Once the connection was made, the heart of Mary was drawn quickly into the extravagant devotional maelstrom.

How did the Church at Rome react to this surge of popular devotion to the anatomically correct human heart of Christ as a burning furnace of love? With reserve, with caution, with a measure of repugnance, with initial resistance to its promotion. But devotees are not easily deterred. When the most devout manifested genuine holiness in their pursuit of the mystery of divine and human love found in the heart of Christ, they eventually found a Roman hearing. [3] Heartfelt devotion and deep piety are often stepping stones to profound conversion. Consider Margaret-Mary Alacoque and John Eudes. Their personal devotion led to popular renewal movements that have persisted into the twentieth century and even to the establishment of new religious orders.

Yet the Roman hierarchy had balked, resisting the

devotional tide as long as it could; it was concerned, notes van Beeck, about "the dangerous turn popular piety might take when encouraged to address prayer to only one portion of Christ, such as the heart," and about "the risk of encouraging further requests for feasts of the eyes, the hands, and the tongue of Jesus."[4] Formal petitions came from hierarchies and religious orders that the Sacred Heart be made an official liturgical feast; these were refused three times in Rome, until 1765, when the matter was conceded first in Poland and then quickly throughout the European Church. Only slowly, suggests van Beeck, did the living Church open itself "to this nervous [cultural] preoccupation with such precious and precarious concerns as life and love."[5] But in order to integrate it within the larger tradition, of liturgical prayer, the devotional impulse had to be purified of its wilder extravagances. Recall the cult of the Sacred Heart as you or your family participated in it in the 1940s and 1950s, and the liturgical celebration of the same mystery each June.

Raymond Firth offers some interesting anthropological reflections on the process by which popular devotion to the Sacred Heart got official approbation.[6] He considered the question in a broader essay asking how once-private symbols feeding personal religious sensibilities and devotions can ever become public symbols for a whole people. Firth observes that whatever symbolic forms successfully cover the distance from the private to the public religious realms will do so only if they speak to fundamental human concerns that are also identified as concerns of the religious authorities who have power to pass judgment on devotional impulses and renewal movements. Firth also shows that in the movement toward official public acceptance of new devotions like the cult of the Sacred Heart religious authorities inevitably discipline the religious sensibilities feeding the cult. Why? So that the new impulses might serve the religious institution's identity and mission. When new religious impulses are embraced within the household of the faith, they are also domesticated.

Annibale Bugnini's dissertation on the history of the liturgy for the feast of the Sacred Heart, from the eighteenth to the twentieth centuries, shows how the human concerns which crystallized in the Sacred Heart devotion were brought into dialogue with the biblical revelation.[7] To summarize what we can learn from the historical process: first, there is the popular devotional impulse converging with a cultural concern; then a popular cult takes shapes to bring the two together; finally there follows the liturgical celebration. Pius XII's encyclical *Haurietis aquas* in 1956 was an *ex post facto* doctrinal capstone on a devotional and liturgical development that had already spanned three centuries.

The history is interesting. But the past is not the point. Our concern is to understand the present. For even as the Church in 1956 was placing its seal on a centuries-long devotional development, restlessness was erupting in the human spirit. Some among us concerned about the mystery of human and divine love were breaking away from known forms, searching about in new places for more adequate symbols of an unquenchable love strong enough to save the world. Why? Perhaps because devotees of the Sacred Heart in Poland, Germany, France, Italy, the United States had just lived through that great concealment of divine love and the massive betrayal of human love that we have come to name "the Holocaust." In the past forty years the whole world has become, with good reason, "nervous" about "life and love."

Yet we are also aware that some among us can still turn to the heart of Mary, as at Medjugorje, where there is assurance that God's love is real, and that we must take heart again in human loving. For these, the now-traditional images of the heart of Christ and the heart of Mary remain adequate. Still, the restless are searching, searching for more adequate symbols to get a better hold on their experiences of God and their own deepest longings. That brings us to look at the stirrings among us at the present.

Honoring the Search

At this point I would like to state my own approach to understanding devotions, renewal movements, and their relationship to the liturgy. I believe those of us concerned about liturgy and its cultural adaptation should attend to the devotional impulses in Catholic life, whether these are manifested in popular cults, novel or traditional, or in renewal movements. Devotional impulses seem to gain intensity at points where liturgy is hard-pressed to meet the peculiar challenges of the dominant culture of the larger society. Where liturgy is resourceless, the people nevertheless supply in some way. Cultural adaptation of the liturgy will follow.

This is a helpful way to understanding what is happening with both the liturgical and the devotional life of the Catholic people of the United States at this juncture in Church renewal. Recall that the Constitution on the Sacred Liturgy makes several recommendations about the renewal of the Church's devotional life that presume a clear and intimate connection between the liturgy and the devotions of the Christian people. But the text as written introduces the value judgment that the liturgy is superior in every way.

Popular devotions of the Christian people are warmly commended. . . . Nevertheless, these devotions should be so drawn up that they harmonize with the liturgical seasons, accord with the sacred liturgy, are in some fashion derived from

it, and lead the people to it, since the liturgy by its very nature far surpasses any of them.[8]

In taking this tone, the Constitution unwittingly gave impe-
tus during the past two decades to the near collapse of devotional practices in the name of liturgical renewal. The truth
of the matter may be that a renewing liturgy responsive
to cultural experience is dependent on a culturally rich
devotional life rather than the other way around.

Professionals who have committed their energies to the
renewal of the liturgy are often befuddled by people's con-
tinued interest in, and perhaps even preference for, the
charismatic renewal, or the program RENEW, or devotions
to Our Lady of Guadalupe, or to saying the Rosary before Sunday Mass. Some Catholics pursue centering prayer;
still others want formal spiritual direction: some seek holistic or creation-centered spirituality. Some go to Christian
feminist gatherings; others want to make traditional pilgrimages. In many dioceses good crowds can be expected
for celebrations in honor of central-American martyr Arch-
bishop Oscar Romero of El Salvador or for the four women
martyrs, Dorothy, Ita, Maura, and Jean. Talking about
the centrality of the Sunday Eucharist in the Christian's
life of prayer may seem futile in the face of the operative
religious sensibilities of the people in our Sunday assemblies.

Imagination, not desperation, is the more appropriate
response for liturgists to bring to such moments. What are
the human concerns to which the popular gatherings and
movements are responding? Liturgy, devotions, and renewal movements within the Church are not separate, parallel streams but currents of the one living water—faith
in the God of Jesus Christ finding expression in our day.
So let me repeat: the devotional impulses in Catholic life,
particularly, should be attended to. These seem to gain

intensity at points where liturgy is hard-pressed to meet
the peculiar challenges of the dominant culture of the larger
society.

Learning from the Case of the Sacred Heart

In order to understand better the relation between contemporary religious impulses and the liturgy, we need to
double back a moment to van Beeck's study to identify some
principles which have bearing on the interpretation of our
contemporary situation. His interest in the Sacred Heart
devotion and its liturgy had come in the context of a con-
sideration of the centuries-long development of the
Christology of the liturgy. He had enunciated as a foundational principle that it is always and inevitably human
concerns which become the names of Christ in the public
prayer of the Church. [9] This has been true from the beginning. When the apostolic generation proclaimed "Jesus is
Lord," it did so concerned to make its commitment in the
face of alternate Jewish and imperial claims and commit-
ments that "YHWH is the Lord, YHWH alone," or that
"Caesar is Lord."

Human concerns, brought to Christ in the obedience
of faith, give rise to Christological language. We can see
this principle illustrated, not only in earlier generations'
naming Jesus "Sacred Heart" and "Lord." We can see it
also in our own day, in the emergence throughout Latin
America of the new naming of Jesus Christ as Liberator.
Our own observations of the searching going on in base
Christian communities in Latin America can help us to ap-
preciate van Beeck's corollary to his foundational principle:
when we worship "in the name of Jesus," making our concerns Christ's names, we are also openly asking Christ to
preside over the concerns of our lives. [10] That means, says
van Beeck, that our concerns, brought to worship, will

have to be tested against the living tradition of the Gospel, disciplined, if necessary, and refined. Inevitably—if not immediately—the tradition of living faith will be enriched and opened up by our cultural concerns, and our cultural concerns will be "corrected and converted" from the self-centeredness in which they arise to become "the stuff of obedience," to use van Beeck's words.

We can find the same principle—of human concerns becoming the names of Christ—illustrated in our current fascination with the discovery that medieval saints of the stature of Anselm of Canterbury, Julian of Norwich, and Bernard of Clairvaux could all pray—happily if quite illogically—to "Jesus, our Mother." What were their concerns, that they prayed in this odd way across three centuries in the high and late Middle Ages? And why did that name "Mother" not become part of the public language of prayer?

Carolyn Walker Bynum's research establishes that for the monks like Anselm and Bernard, at least, theirs was an in-house concern to know that the medieval abbot had a nurturing role in the lives of his brothers. [11] A concern of the cloister remained in the private prayer of the cloister. But Julian, two centuries later, saw a whole Church and world in need of nurture. Did the late medieval pelican iconography carry that concern imaginatively to the Jesus of the Eucharist? Was the concern borne rather by Mary, the Mother of Jesus, named our Mother at the foot of the cross? Certainly the crucifixion iconography that showed suppliants the image of Mary with John standing among patrons and peasants was a standard piece of this period, from which the devout apparently never tired.

As we play imaginatively today with the language of divine motherhood, we have a quite different concern. Ours is about the personhood of women, about the capacity of women to be authentic images of God and full disciples of Christ Jesus, and about women's ability to participate unqualifiedly in his mission to the world. Can our concern become Christ's name? What must we say and do to assure Christ's presidency over our concern? Is the name we search for to express this new concern also "Mother"? Or does the very attraction of the name "mother" say that our concern is only partly about women but largely about caring for the earth and for life itself? According to van Beeck, all human concerns are able to be embraced by Jesus' presidency, and "every human concern is capable of becoming a name of Jesus." But it remains for us to find the rhetoric and the iconography appropriate to our concern.

In this regard Christian feminist gatherings for prayer are absolutely essential if the Christian people are to learn how to pray together in the face of this concern. But they are not the only significant devotional gatherings. All believers who bring cultural concerns to prayer in spontaneous gatherings are important resources for the Church. In such assemblies as these, which play seriously with language and images—stretching the limits of biblical and traditional and ordinary language—new insights will occur. (How did they pray at the August 6–9, 1985, Desert Witness at the Nevada nuclear testing sites just before they committed civil disobedience and so went to jail?) Just as base Christian communities loosened the tongues of inarticulate believers in Latin America and so the whole Sunday assembly has become more eloquent about the liberation which Jesus Christ has accomplished, so also marginal groups are always intermediaries in bringing to the consciousness of the whole Church aspects of the tradition uncelebrated until that time. Many movements of popular piety come and go very quickly. A few, sustained by the faith of believers living through cultural transitions will finally register in the ecclesial tradition as the *sensus fidelium*.

Renewal movements and popular cults exist closest to that growing edge where faith is almost inarticulate, "nervous" about real concerns, intending God while being almost at a loss to name God. At this growing edge, believers can be mistaken; often they cannot yet clearly discern the Spirit. At this growing edge, even when believers' intuitions are sound, they may give uncertain shape and form to experiences of God's presence or of unsatisfied longings for God.

The Gospel presents the matter to us as a problem of knowing what to do with fresh wine. Old skins or new ones? Newer patches on older skins? The history of the Sacred Heart devotion shows us the Carthusians of Cologne in the sixteenth century setting out in a bizarre new direction to present a graphic image of divine and human love; eventually they brought the rest of the Church along. But it ought not to surprise us that the multitudes in every generation will prefer the familiar, what is readily available in the tradition. So thousands travel monthly to Medjugorje to find in Mary the meaning of the deep longings they carry inside themselves. Others who stay at home ask pastors to have holy hours of adoration scheduled again— but now in order to pray for an end to the arms race. Or they want Marian processions to protest the violence of abortion. Patched skins are less risky than losing altogether the wine of longing and desire for the world's salvation because of no skins at all.

On the other hand, neither is it surprising to read a recent report on participation in RENEW in the Milwaukee Archdiocese from 1981 to 1983. Thirty-eight thousand individuals took some part in the movement. What were they after? Maureen Gallagher, co-author of a recent study on the program's participants, offers this reading of the data:

> In catechetical terms, what one sees is the emergence of the desire to form community, to be bonded to a group who share the same interests and faith. The fact that people are experiencing the need for community probably accounts for the success of RENEW.[12]

People close to other institutionalized renewal movements, like the Catholic Charismatic Renewal, Cursillo, and Marriage Encounter, would undoubtedly provide similar testimony, whether scientifically documented or not, that the "greatest strength" of their movement was "community building." The impulse toward human community is an unquestionable religious response to our cultural situation. Auschwitz was a betrayal of human community; so also is apartheid and every other form of genocide, racism, and sexism. Social disintegration confronts people in every direction. Deterrence strategies and Star Wars so-called defense initiatives are only promises for further betrayal.[13]

In such groups as RENEW or the Charismatic Renewal a grassroots impulse for community has already been institutionalized and given some kind of official ecclesiastical approbation. Other grassroots movements for covenanted life together—the Nevada Desert Witness, for example—are less institutionalized, less identified with church structures, have only a vague organizational center and tenuous religious identification, and so are perhaps even closer to the growing edge of contemporary religious sensibilities searching for the center of things.

Attending to Our Own Concerns

Where are we to locate this growing edge of religious concern in our culture? In the United States, where is religious sensibility—the unthematized experience of or longing for God—tapping into cultural crisis? And can our biblical-liturgical tradition help us to name our concern? A whole cluster of disparate activities and movements coalesce around concern for the earth and the future of life upon it—many reflecting what look to others like single-issue craziness. But single issues engage people because they cannot get a good grasp on the whole. Save the whales! Ban the bomb! Bread and roses: The rising of women is the rising of the race! Abortion is murder! As enthusiasts we can be "zealots for bad causes"[14]; we are often also right in our intuitions about where danger, destruction, and blasphemy lie.

Reverence for the earth and reverence for life are fundamental responses to the goodness of God in biblical religion. In the Pentateuch, the cosmos, good and well-ordered to serve human needs, is the sign of the first of the covenants within which humans live. In the tradition of Jewish worship, praise of the author of creation is the starting point of all formal blessing. According to Jacob Neusner, "The three constants in Judaic thinking—creation, revelation, redemption—form the framework in which God as one and unique is confessed and blessed."[15] Yet Western Christians have made celebration of the creator and the covenant within which humans live peacefully on the earth a relatively minor motif in public prayer. Western liturgy, which developed under pressure from the cultural concern with Arianism, has been overshadowed by a profound preoccupation with salvation narrowly understood, with a christomonism rather than a rich trinitarianism.[16]

Certainly the ancient hymns of the Hours tended to celebrate the gifts of light and darkness and the living God who gave the gifts. But in approved English versions of the reformed Roman Hours, even these traditional celebrations of the creator and creation have given way to Christocentric and anthropocentric sentiments. This narrowing was intended as a gain in Christocentric and personalist spirituality. It may be one further unintended step in the continuing disorientation of the Western liturgical tradition.

The disorientation is massive and ancient; it began early and has persisted into the present. Anti-Arianism only reinforced what had already happened. The narrowing shows itself most openly in eucharistic development. Already with Hippolytus in third-century Rome it was congenial for the Christian people to begin the Eucharistic Prayer "in the middle of things" as it were, from a traditional biblical perspective. While the starting point for Eucharistic prayer forms was Jewish euchology, and while this euchology prayed in the order of creation, revelation, redemption, Hippolytus, claiming to be traditional, could start with thanksgiving for the revelation of the forgiveness of sins made in the sacrifice of Jesus, and follow this simply with prayer for the completion of redemption. The creation motif had apparently already atrophied.

From my own reading of Hippolytus, I would argue that the Roman Church had not completely forgotten the praise of the creator by the third century. His "Apostolic Tradition" carried prayers of blessing to be said immediately after the doxology of the great Eucharistic Prayer— blessings celebrating God for the gifts of oil, cheese, and olives. At other times, lights, flowers, and fruit became the occasion for blessing at Rome, if Hippolytus is judged a reliable witness. In a summary statement, Hippolytus wrote, "For everything that is harvested the holy God is to be thanked, and it is to be used for his glory."[17]

Some liturgical theologians have seemed to view the disappearance of the moment of praise for creation as a positive gain or at least no great loss theologically. They imagine the Christian people as having been so over-whelmed by the revelation of Christ's pasch that the Jew-ish protocols for prayer were simply bypassed.[18] This may be the case. But the same suppression of concern for crea-tion did not happen in the Christian orient. In the East, elaborate praise celebrating the creator of the universe and the fruits of creation has been a hallmark of eucharistic praying. Whatever the explanation, and the issues are com-plex, different religious and cultural sensibilities prevailed in the East and West, and we find ourselves today in a Christian West which has felt no need for centuries to inte-grate within its Eucharistic faith both delight in the an-cient covenant of creation and the new covenant of forgiveness of sins.

Years ago Rosemary Haughton wrote perceptively about the formative role of the liturgy. Part of what she said is worth remembering here. She described the rich language of the Church's liturgy, the expressive language of those whose lives had at some moment been opened and transformed by the presence of the living God, as "the lan-guage of conversion."[19] It was the converted who had first uttered the liturgical proclamation "Jesus is Lord." For Haughton, the texts and rites of the liturgical tradition are a storehouse of the language of the converted, available and offered for the use of subsequent generations seeking to name their own experiences of and longings for God. This language of the converted is what gives the liturgy its so-called objective character, since it serves to name, to handle, and to structure the elusive religious experiences of those in every generation who join in the Church's public worship.

But the Western Church suffers acute deprivation in its liturgical heritage precisely at the neuralgic point of our contemporary cultural experience. We simply do not have a developed traditional liturgical language to speak of how care for the earth and for life itself is an integral part of eucharistic faith. Just at the point of our greatest need, we find ourselves at a loss for words, either traditional or contemporary. Yet we desperately need to name this cluster of concerns in our public prayer and to ask Christ to preside over them.

We are so little used to delight in and concern for the earth being voiced as a central Christian religious proclamation that our occasional utterances in public prayer are more redolent of liberal political rhetoric than religious speaking. What has ecology to do with the Eucharist, Catholics begin to wonder. Sensitive to the charge that they had lost their bearings the United States bishops felt compelled to write in *The Challenge of Peace* that their concerns about the nuclear danger were motivated not by any popular movements but by the demands of faith. In biblical language, they warned that for the first time, "creatures have the power to destroy the creation."[20]

Liturgy and the Growing Edges of Faith

So we come to the question: How can liturgists nurture the new cultural-religious sensibility? We are asking a question about development and cultural adaptation for which there is no ready answer. And the development we are talking about has to come in all areas. Our tradition is underdeveloped devotionally as well as liturgically; what buds there are lie dormant.

It is not our purpose or responsibility as liturgists to concern ourselves directly with the promotion of popular piety. The people will find their way. It may well be part of the liturgist's responsibility to be alert to the human concerns which attract people to renewal movements, both cultural and ecclesial. We should also be concerned about the manifestations and the fruits of popular piety and devotion. Judging wheat and chaff requires some criteria for judgment: are these leading to repentance and conversion? to faith, hope, love? to evangelical holiness?

But judging is not nearly so important at this stage as is the presentation of an enlarged biblical viewpoint within which the Church can find its way together. Liturgical commissions can promote this expanding of the religious horizons of the Catholic people in two ways. First, we need to commit ourselves to the affirmation of beauty and the reverence for reality, animate and inanimate, in our liturgical environment and in our Sunday assemblies. The Federation of Diocesan Liturgical Commissions had already identified that agenda; but as a Church we have a long way to go toward honoring it. In my mind the issue is not simply one of aesthetics; it is a matter of religious vision. Our eyes must be opened to the saving truth that human beings are called to live in covenant with the whole earth and the whole cosmos. We must learn to celebrate *that* mystery of our faith with full dedication and growing integrity. People know they hunger for human community. What can we do to deepen awareness that the communion we long for is as wide and wider than the cosmos?

John Dunne, in his recent book *The House of Wisdom*, tells of his discovery of such cosmic faith in an extended visit to Hagia Sophia. [21] He describes well how an architectural form worked its power over him and revealed the mystery of God to him when he opened himself in prayer. The environment brought him to a new level of consciousness, a new relationship with himself, the world, with the living God. American Catholicism has not yet matured to the point of creating a comparable architectural form; perhaps it never will. Meanwhile, we ought to be concerned about the power our places of worship have to form or deform us as human persons in covenant with both earth and cosmos.

Second, we need to look again at the structure of our lectionary and the support it does or does not provide for new religious sensibility and growing piety. The lectionary as currently organized does not give us any room for preaching on the covenants with Adam and Eve and with Noah and his family. Yet the Christian people need to know those stories and to have their truth opened up if they are to understand their own contemporary experiences of longing and desire. Original blessing and primordial sinfulness are not abstractions but valuable interpretative symbols.

Presently, however, the great liturgical narrative of creation is proclaimed annually only at the Easter Vigil. Who preaches on creation on this night? The other major Genesis 1–11 texts appear only in the weekdays of the sixth week of Year I, hardly liturgical prime time. So no actual setting exists for the exploration of these key texts in the Roman liturgy. How can people believe that the way we live on the planet is of ultimate significance if they have not heard? How can they hear if no one preaches to them?

Is promotion of Lectionary reform or of a special indult all that necessary or worthy of the effort of the Federation of Diocesan Liturgical Commissions? I believe it is necessary as a key cultural adaptation of the Roman liturgy to our situation. Cultural concerns impel us to list to the Word of God on covenant living. Only against the backdrop of biblical proclamation of covenanted relationships among God, God's chosen, the earth, and the whole cosmos can we understand and develop appropriate social consciences. Only when we have let the vision of biblical faith form us and convert us can the social doctrine of the United States bishops' pastorals on war and the economy be integrated with Eucharistic faith.[22] We need to return to Genesis and even to some of the apparently obscure laws about reverence for blood elsewhere in the Pentateuch. There is wisdom in Scripture we desperately need if we are to celebrate the Eucharist well. All the treasures of Scripture have not yet been opened to us.

Our religious situation is becoming clearer. We have great concerns about care for the earth and respect for life. We care about woman's reality in the design of human life and community. Yet neither our tradition of popular devotion nor our sacramental-liturgical tradition has developed in such a way as to support and interpret our concerns or to bring us together to deeper conversion. Liturgists cannot do everything to supply for long-standing deficiencies in our outlook as believers. We can do something. There is no easy way to "make up for" a gap in the Western tradition of Eucharistic faith. But we have to begin to live in greater critical awareness of the way our cultural experience is putting our received tradition of Christian worship into question.

In closing we return to Peter Brown's observation:

> The quality of a religious system depends perhaps less on its specific doctrine than on the choice of problems that it regards as important, the areas of human experience to which it directs attention.

To what shall Catholic liturgists now direct their attention these days in the process of the continuing renewal of the Church's public worship?

Notes

1. Frans Josef van Beeck, *Christ Proclaimed: Christology as Rhetoric* (New York: Paulist Press, 1979) 519.

2. *Ibid.* chapter 13, "Two Birds Come to the Mustard Tree," 519–74.

3. *Ibid.* 542ff.; cf. 523ff.; also Raymond Firth. *Symbols: Public and Private* (Ithaca, N.Y.: Cornell University Press, 1973) 230–34.

4. van Beeck, *Christ Proclaimed: Christology as Rhetoric* 523.

5. *Ibid.* 547.

6. Firth, *Symbols: Public and Private* 236–40.

7. Annibale Bugnini, *Cor Jesu. Commentationes in Litteras Encyclicas "Haurietis Aquas,"* I Pars Theologica. (Rome: Herder, 1959) 59–94.

8. *Sacrosanctum Concilium*, no. 13; *The Documents of Vatican II*, Walter Abbott, ed. (New York: America Press, 1966).

9. van Beeck, *Christ Proclaimed: Christology as Rhetoric* 146ff.

10. *Ibid.* 152ff.; also 183.

11. Carolyn Walker Bynum, *Jesus as Mother* (Berkeley: University of California Press, 1982) 112 ff.

12. Maureen Gallagher, "Participation in RENEW: Why and Why Not?" *The Living Light* (June 1985) 322.

13. Patricia Mische, *Star Wars and the State of Our Souls* (East Orange, N.J.: Global Education Associates, 1985).

14. Phrase from the liturgical confession for the Day of Atonement, cited in Jacob Neusner, *The Life of Torah* (Encino, Calif.: Dickinson, 1974) 151.

15. Jacob Neusner, *The Way of Torah: An Introduction to Judaism*, 2nd ed. (Encino, Calif.: Dickinson, 1974) 11–14; 29.

16. Josef Jungmann, *The Place of Christ in Liturgical Prayer*, 2nd rev. ed. (Staten Island: Alba House, 1965) also Cypriano Vagaggini. *Theological Dimensions of the Liturgy* (Collegeville: The Liturgical Press, 1976) 208 ff.

17. Cited in Lucien Deiss, *Springtime of the Liturgy* (Collegeville, The Liturgical Press, 1979) 149.

18. Thomas Talley, "From Berakah to Eucharistia: A Reopening Question," *Worship* 50:2 (March 1976) 136.

19. Rosemary Haughton, *The Transformation of Man: A Study of Conversion and Community* (New York: Paulist Press, 1967) 245 ff; 268–80.

20. United States Catholic Conference, "The Challenge of Peace: God's Promise and Our Response," *Origins* 13:1 (May 19, 1983) 30.

21. John Dunne, *The House of Wisdom* (San Francisco: Harper and Row, 1985) 26–54.

22. In both the peace and economic pastorals, the USCC has provided expansive bases in a biblical theology of covenant to undergird the Church's social doctrine.

4

The Arts: Language of the Spirit

LOUIS WEIL

I begin with an extraordinary poem. It is called "The Bright Field" and was written by the Welsh poet R. S. Thomas.

> I have seen the sun break through
> to illuminate a small field
> for a while, and gone my way
> and forgotten it. But that was the pearl
> of great price, the one field that had
> the treasure in it. I realize now
> that I must give all that I have
> to possess it. Life is not hurrying
> on to a receding future, nor hankering after
> an imagined past. It is the turning
> aside like Moses to the miracle
> of the lit bush, to a brightness
> that seemed as transitory as your youth
> once, but is the eternity that awaits you.[1]

This poem says everything that I want to say to you, and it says it through an instrument that is far better suited to our subject than the formal lecture I am about to give.

But the form of a lecture is the instrument available to me, and I use it acutely aware of its limitations. I shall be using concepts and words to point toward deeply-felt meanings that operate into a dimension beyond the capacities of language.

The Inclusive "Scope of Aesthetic Experience"

I want to speak to you about experience. Although we are concerned with the arts, I hesitate to use the phrase "aesthetic experience" because for many that will suggest an elitism which I do not intend. That would be an easy trap for me to fall into. The fine arts have played and continue to play a significant role in my life. That is not a common ground for everyone, however, and in matters concerning worship we need a common ground quite simply because our worship is the expression of a common faith which calls into unity persons of widely divergent aesthetic experiences and tastes, not to mention cultural backgrounds. When an elitist speaks of "good taste," that is usually a reference to his own taste. I want to avoid trivializing what I am trying to say should I seem to be taking one dimension—aesthetic experience—to be the whole.

Yet I have to be faithful to my own personal history, and it is beauty that led me to faith. Now I find that, some thirty years later, after spending a great deal of time and energy on intellectual aspects of the Christian enterprise, it is still beauty which offers me the framework in which all the other dimensions are brought together in integration. In those three decades, my sense of the scope of aesthetic experience has greatly expanded. If the fine arts were for me the means of access to this realm—the realm of faith—I now see them as an important clue, a sign of the extraordinary ways in which sensual experience opens our perceptions to realities beyond the capacities of human reasoning. This is not a confession of despair, nor a public admission that I have become an anti-intellectual. But I am expressing a deep conviction that in worship, Christian faith is engaged in a holistic way in which all dimensions of our humanity are involved.

My first experiences of being engaged in this total way were, as I have implied, through contact with great works of art, especially, in my case, through music. It was for me very much what T. S. Eliot has described: "You are the music while the music lasts."[2] But now I know that this type of experience is by no means limited to the domain of the fine arts. R. S. Thomas speaks of an experience in nature, seeing "the sun break through to illuminate a small field," yet an experience which is revelatory of the whole, a sign of "the pearl of great price, the one field that had the treasure in it."

I would want to use the phrase "aesthetic experience" to embrace both these types of human experience, both that domain which we are thinking of when we say "the arts," and also the response to nature, and to all other dimensions of human experience in which our senses are engaged. Undoubtedly more careful defining is needed, but I want to use "aesthetic experience" in this inclusive way because the arts so often open to us the doors of a deeper perception, revealing a self-authenticating quality which is beyond the power of language to define.

The Fundamental Role of Beauty

When he accepted the Nobel Prize for literature in 1970, Aleksandr Solzhenitsyn quoted Dostoevsky's mysterious remark: "Beauty will save the world."[3] Whereas truth and goodness can be perverted for purposes not their own, beauty remains sovereign, elusive, unpredictable, free.

Beauty does not replace truth and goodness, but is their indispensable complement if they are not to become rigidified within narrowly cognitive systems and thus to betray their highest intentions. Solzhenitsyn concludes his comments with words which reflect the agony of his own experience:

> So perhaps the old tri-unity of Truth, Goodness, and Beauty is not simply the decorous and antiquated formula it seemed to us at the time of our self-confident materialistic youth. If the tops of these three trees do converge, as thinkers used to claim, and if the all too obvious and the overly straight sprouts of Truth and Goodness have been crushed, cut down, or not permitted to grow, then perhaps the whimsical, unpredictable and ever surprising shoots of Beauty will force their way through and soar up to *that very spot*, thereby fulfilling the task of all three?[4]

In a lecture on the place of beauty in theology, Canon A. M. Allchin comments that Solzhenitsyn's words are "an affirmation which makes very high claims for the artist, . . . that art has an essential part to play in saving humankind, in assuring the continuing identity of man as a creature who can know and love what is good, what is true, what is beautiful, and whose being can only find its fulfillment when that love and knowledge are fused together into a single movement of celebration and delight."[5] This use of the word "celebration" will inevitably suggest—at least I hope it will suggest!—some link between all this and what liturgy is about. In the perspective of Allchin's comment, dare we claim that the liturgy is that point of fusion where all the dimensions of our humanity are brought "together into a single movement of celebration" which is nothing less than a universal oblation?

If beauty plays so fundamental a role, why has its significance received so little attention, at least not in the theo-

logical writings of the past few centuries. As Allchin goes
on to say,

> The saving power of beauty is not a subject treated in most
> text-books of dogmatics. Theological reflection on man's rela-
> tionship with God as the source of his identity and being has
> concentrated on the ethical and the philosophical realms, not
> on the aesthetic.

Only in very recent years, in the work of Hans Urs von
Balthasar, has there been some recovery of the role of
beauty within theological reflection. As he says, beauty
"will not allow herself to be separated and banned from
her two sisters (i.e. truth and goodness) without taking
them along with herself in an act of mysterious
vengeance."[6]

I think, however, that this separation of beauty which
has been so characteristic of theological reflection can be
easily understood, since, as Allchin comments, "beauty remains sovereign, elusive, unpredictable, free." Those are
threatening characteristics to a dogmatic mind-set. Where
might beauty lead us? Upon what uncharted paths? I am
reminded of an occasion some years ago when I preached
on Pentecost, and spoke in reference to the tenth anniversary of the death of Pope John XXIII. In that sermon, I
quoted a wonderful phrase from St. Athanasius in which
he images the Son and the Holy Spirit as the right and left
hands of God. If the Incarnation affirms God's participation in the human order and can be seen as a foundation
for the legitimacy of institutional structures as instruments
of God's purpose, Pentecost and the outpouring of the Holy
Spirit remind us that "the Spirit of God blows where it
wills," and that a theology of the Holy Spirit must involve
God's freedom, God's sovereignty over institutional structures, God's unpredictability in regard to the accomplish-
ment of his purposes. To speak of these aspects of the Spirit's

activity is, of course, to draw upon Solzhenitsyn's asser-
tions about beauty, and this is not an artificial link. What
I am concerned about in our attempts to speak of the
Spirit's activity is precisely in this realm of what we might
call the creative dimensions of the Church's life—the uncharted, the unpredictable, what seems to emerge from
a kind of spontaneous energy, and to bubble forth, fresh
and new.

It would require an arrogance beyond my wildest
presumption to suggest that I am presenting a systematic
theology of the Holy Spirit, but I am trying to assert a particular dimension of such a theology which strikes me as
important and not adequately perceived. The epicletic
character of Christian liturgy suggests a constant enliven-
ing of ecclesial structures and liturgical patterns by the free
activity of the Spirit, whose creative activity involves the
begetting of new life, new images, new perceptions. In this
perspective, the activity of the Spirit is very closely related
to what I have suggested to be the fundamental role of the
arts, the arts, that is, in a very inclusive sense. The Spirit
is the generator, the source of all the creative energies with
which the Christian community is gifted.

Yet the reality of our past history has been marked by
the suppression of this creativity for the sake of a hallowed
model, for which the arts were tamed and eventually
trivialized. Inevitably, the truly fresh, creative energies of
the arts moved apart as aliens to the faith which should
have fostered their integration and nurture.

A great deal of research in this century has helped to
illuminate our understanding of the cultural, social, and
even political factors which led the Church into the theological and institutional structures quite familiar to us all.
But for those of us whom the Church calls to special responsibility for the shaping of the corporate worship of Chris-

tian communities, it is urgent that we recognize the impact of this heritage upon common perceptions about the liturgy. The response to the revision of liturgical rites is an adequate indication of the fixity of mentality which dominated Christian attitudes and experience. Shortly before his death in 1971, the English writer Philip Toynbee commented that "Christians should recognize . . . that their traditional theology was the very peculiar product of a very peculiar historical period."[7] Yet it is precisely this theology, this highly polished cognitive enterprise, which radically shaped our fundamental attitudes toward the nature of Christian worship, fixed the norms of that worship within canonically controlled formularies, and defended the purity of this ritual pattern from the impact of the diversity and richness of other cultures as the Church's missionary activity carried its witness into situations which might have challenged its understanding of the Gospel to become incarnate in these new cultural contexts. There were, of course, some missionaries, such as Mateo Ricci in China, who sought ways in which Christ might be proclaimed within the forms of another culture. In our own century Raimundo Pannikar and Anskar Chupungo have confronted us with this same imperative.

Yet on the whole such adaptation and the creativity which it generates find no significant place in the Church's agenda, whatever particular tradition one may want to name. I was recently involved as a consultant in the preparation of the French version of the new American Book of Common Prayer. The guidelines were carefully set before us: the French version was to be a translation, adhering faithfully to the authorized English language text; adaptation was not acceptable. When this approach landed the commission in liturgical absurdity, each exception to the rule had to be carefully and forcefully argued.

This institutional rigidity is particularly difficult for us who are sensitive to the fact that the official models are themselves very much the product of a particular culture, and were thus inevitably generated from within its own norms of cultic language and ritual action. My point is not to denigrate the aesthetic quality of Gothic architecture or plainsong or any other aspects of the artistic heritage of the Western Church. The problem lies in the fixing of any such models as normative for the Church's worship for every culture and in every age. In the establishment of such models as "normative," the fresh springs of creativity are effectively excluded from the liturgical act, and rites come to be celebrated more as the repetition of static models than as ever-new encounters between God and the community of faith. [8]

Stewards of the Mysteries of God

The traditional ordination rite of the Anglican Prayer Book tradition refers to the new priest as a "steward of the mysteries." Although the new rite does not keep this phrase, I think that its meaning is important. We are stewards of the mysteries of God, not the custodians of museum treasures. It is appropriate, of course, for the Church in its concern for unity to see in the liturgy a significant sign of that unity. The Church cannot as an institution relinquish oversight of these matters, yet the character of that oversight will have serious impact upon the local community's experience of the liturgical act. Although I shudder to think what might be perpetrated in our parishes if, for example, Episcopal priests were expected to create new liturgical forms each week, this cannot be justification for binding the liturgical act in canonical chains. If we may judge from the text of *Apostolic Tradition*, it was already being recognized by the early third century that not all clergy have the gift for spontaneous prayer. But the liturgy is a multi-faceted action with a wide range of dimensions in which the creative gifts of the community may find voice.

This is not merely the complaint of someone for whom the arts are important, and I certainly recognize that whenever we move in this more open direction, a great deal more work is required than when a liturgical rite is celebrated, as it were, from a can, that is, according to a very fixed model. My real concern touches a much more fundamental level, namely, the nature of the liturgical act as a focus to the experience of faith. I am back to my word "experience," and it is there that I want to speak of what is for me an essential connection between aesthetic experience and liturgical experience, where the nature of aesthetic experience illuminates, I believe, the intention of liturgical experience.

When I experience a work of art (and here I am using the fine arts as a point of departure), the meaning of that experience lies within the experience itself. The value, for example, of my looking at El Greco's painting of the resurrection is not that it teaches me data about the resurrection. It is not essentially a cognitive experience. Rather, it is a holistic experience in which my entire being is engaged. Similarly, I do not listen to Mozart because this will shape my moral attitudes. When I give myself over to a work of art, there is an encounter with reality which is self-authenticating, absolutely convincing, and yet not subject to definition in words or mathematical formulas.

I am suggesting that this type of experience, what I have called in general and inclusive terms the "aesthetic experience," is essentially the same as that which is offered to us in the liturgical act. The Church is thus, in the liturgy, the steward of an encounter with the Holy One. Just as a performer does not *control* the nature of the experience of each listener, so the Church's role, or more particularly that of the clergy and other liturgical ministers, is not to control the experience, but rather to be stewards of it, much as in concert a pianist enables the aesthetic experience of the audience, but at the same time enters into it and shares it as a participant. I am concerned about this latter point because those of us who have particular liturgical responsibility in the Church are not charlatans involved in the manipulation of a determined effect. We are ourselves members of the family of faith. We may be stewards of this encounter with the Holy, but we are stewards of what we see as God's initiative of grace toward the community of believers.

Our sense of the liturgy as encounter, that the meaning is in the liturgical action and not in some derived effect, has often become obscured. Participation in the liturgy has been seen in terms of obedience to the Church's law, or the way in which grace is obtained to live one's daily life. Such dimensions, however, are not at the heart of the matter. The nurture of faith through Word and sacrament is not accomplished through some cognitive assimilation. Rather, in the fragile forms of the liturgy, as in the fragile forms of other persons, we encounter the living Lord. The God who is beyond all created forms meets us in the immediacy of this celebration of our faith. The meaning is found in the doing; the meaning is known in the experience—but known in an all-encompassing way.

Perhaps this is why the fundamental liturgical action is based upon the command of Jesus to "do this." Faith is not a once and for all matter or else it stagnates and dies. It is nourished and grows in these repeated doings in which we find our faith confirmed not merely at the rational level, but in our whole being. As in the aesthetic experience, the meaning of the liturgical experience is in the doing. A story is told—perhaps apocryphal—about Martha Graham. In a workshop she performed a solo dance, and then a participant asked her what it meant, and she repeated the dance. In words she could have said a great deal about dance, its history, theory, whatever, but the meaning of the dance was what only the dance itself could express. So also for us. We can all talk a great deal about the liturgy, from many different aspects, but the meaning of the liturgy is found only in the liturgical act itself. That meaning is the mysterious action of God. We are stewards of the forms in which that action takes human and visible shape. For the members of our various communities, characterized as we are by widely different resources, the liturgical experience is the focus of encounter with God. To pick up again on the images of R. S. Thomas's poem, can we enable this experience to be "the turning aside . . . to the miracle of the lit bush"?

The liturgy can be such an experience in a wide range of styles. When I use the model of aesthetic experience, I do not want to be misunderstood to mean that the experience of the Holy requires a magnificent building, glorious music, and the whole panoply of movement, colors, and smells. There are, of course, those occasions when the use of splendid resources is appropriately called forth from the community. [9] But I am suggesting an expansion of our understanding of the arts to include the entire complex of human crafts, all those physical dimensions for which we are stewards, and about which choices are made within a given context. In this expanded view, "the arts" would include a wide diversity of artifacts which are produced from the whole range of national cultures and by the varieties of human creative gifts.

The whole created, physical world is the resource for the Church's liturgical experience. Wherever men and women draw upon the resources offered by nature, and bring to these resources their human skills, it is, I believe, appropriate to speak in some sense of *art*. This is not to suggest that there can be no criteria for evaluation or judgment. Some of this world of art may have limited expressive power. But I do suggest that if we are to begin to come to grips in any adequate way with the relation of the arts to worship, we must first perceive the kinship between aesthetic and religious experience, and that will open our perception to a whole world of artistic expression from within our local communities and from cultures quite different from our own.

Many years ago, in Haiti, a group of artists approached a bishop to ask if they might paint a mural in a newly-built educational building. Unfortunately, and this was many years ago, the bishop had been formed within the narrowly-defined models of which I spoke earlier. He refused their request, and by way of explanation said, "the Church has its art." Since that incident, much of Haitian art has been recognized as among the most powerful spiritual expressions of this century. If the liturgical experience is to be an encounter with the Holy, the physical context in which it takes place cannot evoke another culture without suggesting that there are parts of the created world that do not belong to God. When a particular community of faith brings its gifts into the context of its corporate praise, the particular will speak of the whole, and the whole creation will be claimed as the context of the Church's thanksgiving. The language of the Spirit speaks with countless voices: the liturgical act as the experience of the Church's faith invites us to draw all those voices into a common offering of praise.

Notes

1. *Laboratories of the Spirit,* in *Later Poems, 1972–1982* (London: Macmillan, 1983) 81.

2. "The Dry Salvages," V, in *Four Quartets* (London: Faber, 1944).

3. Said by Ippolit to Prince Myshkin in *The Idiot* (1868) part III, chapter 5; cf. "Nobel Lecture," in *Aleksandr Solzhenitsyn: Critical Essays and Documentary Materials.* J. B. Dunlop, R. Haugh, and A. Klimoff, eds. (New York: Collier, 1975) 559.

4. *Ibid.,* 560.

5. Unpublished manuscript.

6. *The Glory of the Lord. A Theological Aesthetics,* vol. I: *Seeing the Form* (San Francisco: Ignatius, 1982) 18.

7. *Towards the Holy Spirit* (London: SCM Press, Ltd., 1981) 26, item 64.

8. Cf. my essay, "Liturgical Creativity," in *Parish: A Place for Worship,* Mark Searle, ed. (Collegeville: The Liturgical Press, 1981) 81–96.

9. Cf. my article, "The Liturgy on Great Occasions: Notes on Large-Scale Celebrations," *Living Worship* (February 1978) vol. 14, no. 2.

Authors

GERARD AUSTIN, O.P. is chairman of the department of theology at The Catholic University of America. His doctorate in theology is from the Institut Catholique in Paris, where he also received the Magister Sacrae Liturgiae.

He has published articles in *Ephemerides Liturgicae, Scriptorium, New Catholic Encyclopedia, New Catholic World, Worship, American Ecclesiastical Review,* and *Pastoral Music.* He is the author of *Anointing With the Spirit: The Rite of Confirmation* published by Pueblo Publishing Company in 1985.

He is a past-president of the North American Academy of Liturgy and is a member of the National Southern Baptist/Roman Catholic Scholars' Dialogue and the Bishops' Committee on the Liturgy's Subcommittee on the Lectionary.

MARY COLLINS, O.S.B. is the former prioress of Holy Wisdom Monastery in Wake Forest, N.C. She is also past president of the North American Academy of Liturgy and associate professor in the department of religion and religious education at The Catholic University of America (on leave 1985-86).

Her doctorate is from The Catholic University of America. She has published "Daughters of the Church: The Four Theresas" in *Women—Invisible in Theology and Church* (1986). She has also authored "Naming God in Public Prayer," *Worship* (July 1985).

She serves on the advisory board of the International Commission on English in the Liturgy, is a past-president of The Liturgical Conference (1975-80), and is co-director (with David Power) of the Liturgy issue of *Concilium.*

THERESA F. KOERNKE, I.H.M. is assistant professor of theology at Mt. St. Mary Seminary/Athenaeum of Ohio in Cincinnati. Her doctorate is from the University of Notre Dame.

She is the author of "The Sacred Liturgy: Toward the Fullness of Human Existence," an article in the book *Remembering the Future: Vatican II and Tomorrow's Liturgical Agenda,* published by Paulist Press in 1983.

She also serves on the board of trustees of Marygrove College in Detroit and is director of religious education for the Romanian Byzantine Catholic Exarchate in the United States.

LOUIS WEIL is professor of liturgy at Nashotah House in Wisconsin. His doctorate in theology is from the Institut Catholique in Paris.

He is the author of *Liturgy for Living*, published by Seabury, and *Sacraments and Liturgy: The Outward Signs*, published by Blackwell.